# KNOSSOS
## AND THE
## HERAKLEION MUSEUM

### BRIEF ILLUSTRATED
### ARCHAEOLOGICAL GUIDE

**COSTIS DAVARAS**
Ephor of Antiquities

**ATHENS**

**EDITIONS HANNIBAL**

**Cover plate (on the front)**
**Museum of Herakleion**

*The «Ladies in blue». Fresco from Knossos.*

**Cover plate (on the back)**

*Grand Staircase of the East Wing: The "Veranda of the Royal Guard". In the background a replica of the fresco with figure-of-eight shields.*

*Translated by*
**ALEXANDRA DOUMAS**

*Photographs by*
**HANNIBAL**

*Supervision of printer's proofs*
**ELEFTHERIA KONDYLAKI**

*Colour reproductions*
**CHRISTOS ANTONIADES**

*Phototypeset by*
**FOTRON A.S.**

*Printed by*
**EKTYPOTIKE**

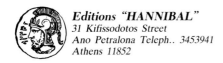

*Editions "HANNIBAL"*
*31 Kifissodotos Street*
*Ano Petralona Teleph.. 3453941*
*Athens 11852*

# THE PALACE OF KNOSSOS

## General Survey

The epicentre of the refined Minoan civilisation of the palatial period, which flourished in Crete during the 2nd millennium BC and was one of the great civilisations of the ancient world, are the four palaces: Knossos, Phaistos, Mallia and Zakros. These impressive edifices were built in around 1900 BC in geographically apposite locations, ensuring direct connection with the rich rural hinterland and the important sea routes of the Aegean and Mediterranean. Smaller "palaces" existed too, seat of the local governor, such as that at Gournia. The palaces were both the creation and necessity of a centralised economy and social organisation, apparently headed by a "Priest king" of which the legendary Minos, known from classical Greek tradition, was the prototype. It has also been suggested that the several palaces presuppose several kings, certainly without any mutual political rivalry and probably with some degree of independence, under the hegemony of the king of Knossos who may have had a religious supremacy. Whatever the case, the leading role of Knossos in religion, as well as in the island's administration, legislature and economy is quite obvious.

The large palaces served many purposes. They should not be compared with those of recent times and regarded only as the residence of the king, his family, courtiers, artists and other servant personnel, as well as functioning as the axis of the sophisticated life of a highly stratified society such as that of prehistoric Crete surely was. The Minoan palaces, surrounded by opulent villas and an extensive urban community were also the seat of administration and justice, as well as important commercial and manufacturing centres and nodes of control of the economic and productive activities of a wider area. Stored in the palaces' vast magazines were not only goods destined for local consumption by their royal and other residents, but mainly produce for redistribution and trade, income from "taxes" which were, of course, levied in kind since money was still unknown. The palaces were at the same time workshops, for all significant forms of art were produced there.

Equally significant was the religious role played by the palaces. Their west wings in particular were dedicated to the cult of the Mother Goddess, but there were religious elements everywhere and the palaces were simultaneously major shrines and centres of religious life, ceremonies and rituals.

The architecture of the Minoan palaces owes something to the enormous temple-palaces of the East. A common feature is the rectangular central court, though in Crete this is not delimited by rectilinear external walls. On the contrary, the Minoan palace developed from the inside outwards, starting from the large court which comprised its structural focus as well as being the axis of its entire life. Thus the external facades frequently terminated in butts and recesses. In general we should bear in mind that although the basic plan of the palaces had been conceived of from the outset in detail, its final form was in a way the natural outcome of a long evolutionary process with successive buildings and numerous architectural phases. The walls were covered with plaster decorated with paintings in the most important rooms. Built square pillars were frequently used for support, as well as round wooden columns characteristically tapering towards the base. These peculiar columns, a diagnostic feature of Minoan architecture, basically consisted of upside-down tree trunks, this inversion preventing the possibility of them sprouting and also protecting the base from the rain.

The palaces were destroyed several times but were rebuilt after each catastrophe. In all they stood for some six hundred years. Two principal architectural phases can be distinguished: the Early Palaces which were destroyed in around 1700 BC, perhaps by violent earthquakes, and the new Palaces which were erected on the same site. Eventually these too were destroyed in circa 1450 BC along with most of the other towns and villages of Crete, but the palace of Knossos suffered less serious damage than the others. There are signs here that after the disaster a new dynasty of Achaean kings was installed. They were Greek-speaking and ruled Crete along the same lines as a Mycenaean kingdom. This period lasted until the final catastrophe, a conflagration in the palace, dated to about 1375 BC or even later. The Achaean dynasty apparently disappeared and the site was never rebuilt or reused as a palace.

The largest palace in Crete was at Knossos, built upon the ruins of an extensive and very important Neolithic settlement. It was more or less square, of side 150 metres, and covered an area of 20,000 sq. m. All around was a large town with a population estimated as comparable with that of present-day Herakleion, though Hood thinks it was much smaller. Neither the town nor the palace were protected by fortification walls, a unique phenomenon for that era, since there was no threat of internal war or external invasion, for the sea was well guarded by Minos' fleet. At that time Crete, though small in area and population, became the first naval power in world history and the "Thalassocracy" of Minos has remained legendary.

The complex plan of the palace of Knossos and the fact that the double axe (labrys), the most sacred symbol of Minoan religion, is incised many times on walls and pillars, prompted the notion that this building was the labyrinth, dwelling place of the labrys. A recently discovered Linear B tablet (ill. 65) has disclosed the existence of a cult title "My Lady of the Labyrinth". After the palace's destruction the ruins were even more labyrinthine in appearance and so the specific meaning of the word was derived, which passed from Greek to Latin and so into most of the modern European languages.

Knossos survived in later Greek times as one of the mighty city-states of Dorian Crete. Traditional subjects such as the labyrinth and the Minotaur were depicted on its coinage.

Following a preliminary excavation in 1878 by the Herakliote antiquarian Minos Kalokairinos, the palace was systematically explored by the English archaeologist Sir Arthur Evans and his collaborators from 1900 to 1905. Work has been continued intermittently ever since by the British School of Archaeology.

# Visit to the Palace

The palace is built on a levelled hilltop (ill. 7) which is not so obvious nowadays because the west slope has been covered with infill from the excavation. The visitor first enters the West Court (ill. 10), a large paved area resting on an outer retaining wall with a broad ramp to the west, forming the entrance. At the far end stands the monumental west facade of the palace, its massive blocks blackened by the great fire which destroyed the building for the last time. In the West Court there are three enormous circular pits with built walls, resembling three shallow wells, known as "kouloures", In the two westernmost "kouloures" traces of Protopalatial houses were found, one of which had a flight of red plastered stairs and was surely of a religious character. These early dwellings were obsoleted when the court and "kouloures" were made. There are similar "kouloures" in the palace of Mallia also. Their function is uncertain, though they were probably originally granaries and not cisterns. In a later phase the discarded broken pottery from the palace was thrown into them. The court is traversed by slightly raised causeways which were probably used for sacred processions and other ceremonies or simply as pathways. There are also two altars. One is built in front of the monumental west facade, perhaps on the site of the original entrance to the Early Palace which was blocked in the course of subsequent remodelling of the facade. The foundations of the Early Palace are still visible as a row of large flagstones in the pavement of the court. Maybe the altar was built here because the space between the earlier and later facade was considered holy.

A "causeway" across the court leads to the west entrance of the palace, the West Propylon. This porch had a large wooden column of estimated height 5.50 m. standing on an alabaster base and a wall-painting of bull-sports on its east wall. Next to it was a guard lodge and reception room which perhaps contained a throne for the duty officer controlling the entrance. Behind a double door at the far end of the porch begins the long Corridor of the Procession (ill. 9). This was a ceremonial entrance, thus named after the wall-painting which adorned the corridor walls in two superimposed zones consisting of figures of boys and girls, estimated as several hundred, forming a procession. Some of the youths were playing musical instruments and clad in sacerdotal robes. The central figure of the wall-painting represented a goddess.

The "Cup bearer" (ill. 13) is especially famous, sun-tanned, curly-haired, broad-shouldered and slim-waisted, he is a typical Minoan. The youth holds a heavy conical rhyton of stone, a special libation vessel, and wears a seal-stone around his left wrist. The Corridor of the Procession, which is only preserved for part of its length, skirts the southwest corner of the palace and the small South Entrance, leading eventually to the South Propylon (ill. 12), a magnificent columned structure with three entrances closed by doors. As with the other frescoes in the palace, a replica of part of the wall-painting of the procession has been placed in the restored Porch (ill. 11) which originally covered a significant part of it. The propylon, paved with large flagstones, and the so-called Grand Straircase, bordered by strong walls and colonnades, led from the ground floor to the first floor, known as the piano nobile, an architectural term borrowed from the Italian Renaissance (ill.8). On this floor is a series of formal rooms, almost completely restored, including the "Tricolumnar Shrine", "Great Hall" with two columns, "Sanctuary Hall" with six columns and other chambers with conventional names (ill. 14). Evans claimed that there was a Greek temple, probably dedicated to the goddess Rhea, to the east of the Grand Staircase, though his evidence was scant and it was demolished in the course of the excavations. Next to the south entrance is a copy of the well-known relief fresco of the "Priest-king" or "Prince of the Lilies" (ill. 16). According to a recent study this rich yet simply clad figure with bare torso and crown or diadem with standing lilies surmounted by three large backward-trailing peacock plumes constitutes, unfortunately, an erroneous reconstitution of fresco fragments belonging to three different figures, two boxers and a priestess, who wore the lily crown.

Leading to the palace south entrance was an impressive structure known as the Stepped Portico (ill. 17) which belonged to the Protopalatial period and has left very few traces. There were columns on its west side only, while there was a high blank wall to the east. In order to enter the portico and palace one had to pass over a large monumental viaduct with stepped channels. The road to southern Crete and the Libyan Sea commenced here. A small building at the roadside was probably intended as a hostellery for travellers and was called the "Caravanserai" (ill. 20) by the excavators.

There is a well and large public footbath of stone, in which the water still runs, in the "Caravanserai". Of considerable importance is a wall-painting which adorned the upper part of a wall, a frieze of partridges and hoopoes (ill.21). Even further south, again at the roadside, stands the large royal "Temple-tomb" (ill. 18, 19) a two-storeyed building with court and hypostyle crypt. In the centre of the rock-cut burial chamber stands a square pillar.

The large Central Court of the palace (ill. 22) covers an area of 50×25m. Beneath its original pavement various remains of the Neolithic settlement at Knossos have been exavated. The ground floor of the west wing was principally intended for religious purposes. At the north edge is the Throne Room (ill. 23). Passing through a foor-door polythyron or pier and door partition, one descends five steps into an antechamber with gypsum benches around the walls. Between the benches along the north wall a wooden replica of the stone throne from the Throne Room itself has been placed on the exact spot where a heap of charred material was found. This lobby was decorated with wall-paintings. A porphyry basin found nearby has been placed in the centre of it, in its putatively original position. Perhaps this basin was for holy water (ill. 24). The Throne Room proper, which has two entrances, lies to the west and against its north wall stands the renowned "throne of Minos" (ill. 23) which was discovered perfectly preserved and "in situ". Made of gypsum it clearly imitates a wooden prototype. The hollows in the seat were for greater comfort. The splendid high back has an undulating outline and slopes slightly back-wards. The throne was covered with a thin coat of red and white painted plaster. There are benches to right and left of it while the wall above was embellished with murals of wingless griffins flanking the throne; fabulous sacred monsters with lion's body and eagle's head, attendants of the deities and guardians of sacred places and objects with were inherited by later Greek mythology and art. These wall-paintings display a rudimentary application of chiaroscuro. Two similar griffins adorn the other walls. This throne, popularly known as the "oldest in Europe" was perhaps not infact intended for Minos but for a High Priestess of the Mother Goddess. Opposite and at a lower lever is a "lustral basin" access to which was by six steps and which was surely for ritual purifications with holy water. Similar lustral basins exist elsewhere in the palace, as well as in the other palaces and villas. Some archaeologists consider them to be ordinary baths, yet they have no drainage system. This lustral basin had a low parapet of wooden columns, as is deduced from charred traces, and formed the lower part of a light well. The upper parts of the walls were covered with red plaster. The Throne Room and its wall-paintings date perhaps to the period of the Achaean dynasty. The archaeological evidence suggests that some ceremony was being performed here at the very moment of the destruction of the palace and was abruptly interrupted. Perhaps this religious rite was aimed at averting the imminent disaster. West of the Throne Room was a suite of small, dark rooms comprising the so-called "Inner Sanctuary".

Returning to the Central Court and proceeding southwards we come to an impressive staircase with twelve treads and two large columns, one taller than the other, which led directly from the court to the first floor (ill.25). After the staircase and opposite the centre of the court are the ruins of the Tripartite Shrine which was crowned by Horns of Consecration. The central section of the shrine was higher than the lateral ones. This peculiar shrine, which was, in effect, just a facade, is depicted in one of the miniature frescoes from the palace. Still further south we descend into a small paved court which communicates to the north with the "Magazine of the Tall Pithos" (ill.27), and the Temple Repositories. Here, among the treasures of the Tripartite Shrine kept in two rectangular cists sunk in the ground like stone chests, various precious cult objects were revealed; the famous snake goddesses and other exceptional works of art in faience, as well as a large marble cross, a well-known solar symbol. Two doorways on the west side of the paved court lead into two dark, mysterious hypostyle crypts or Pillar Crypts (ill. 26) of indisputably religious character. Each crypt had a large square pillar on which the sacred symbol of the double axe is incised several times. Libations were poured at the base of these pillars which were an aniconic representation of the divinity and their cult is a very well-known feature of Minoan religion. Perhaps a relationship exists with the age-old worship in caves or even with the fact that the pillar crypts were an integral element in the stability of a building in a land which suffered from devastating earthquakes. North of the first crypt there are two other dark chambers: the eastern one has been named the "Vat Room".

Behind the suite of cult rooms in the West Wing extends the row of Magazines (ill.29), the largest unit of storerooms in Minoan Crete. In front of it there is a long corridor which had a wooden roof at the beginning and runs parallel with the Central Court. There are eighteen long narrow magazines in all, with pithoi set on stone bases and rectangular chest-like cists set in the floor, within which clothing and diverse precious objects were kept. In some of the magazines the roof has been restored with cement. These extensive storerooms housed a great number of pithoi, perhaps 420, and are indicative of the role played by the palaces in the economic life of the island, in the trading and redistribution of produce. When the palace was destroyed the burning oil in the pithoi left the greasy black traces still visible on the gypsum slabs. There were pithoi in the corridor too, as well as chests coated internally with plaster for the storage of liquids.

On the other side of the Central Court is the East Wing of the palace with the royal apartments. Whereas the West Wing consisted of the ground floor and two upper storeys, the East Wing had four storeys, since it was set into a deep cutting in the hillside two storeys deeper than the level of the court. Intercommunication between the ground floor, the floors of the royal quarters and the Central Court was facilitated by the Grand Staircase (ill. 30), a truly monumental achievement of Minoan architecture with a capacious light-well to the east, the colonnades of which stood on a stepped parapet. There were verandahs around the other two sides of the light-well, while on the southern one there was a window instead of columns. The broad steps are shallow and very easy to negotiate. The Grand Staircase was preserved more or less intact during excavation, protected inside the deep cutting into the slope. At the far end of the lightwell is the Hall of the Colonnades (ill. 31) with four massive columns. Beyond this a corridor commences in the middle of which was a door as is deduced from the use marks left on the paved floor. The corridor leads to one of the larger rooms in the palace, the Hall of the Double Axes (ill. 39), thus named after this sacred symbol which was carved several times on the walls of the light-well to the west. The Hall is divided by a polythyron and there was a throne on its north wall, possibly with a canopy above, affixed to four fluted wooden colonnettes. The throne was, in all likelihood, of the same type as encountered previously. There was a gypsum dado around the walls and above this they were plastered and painted with spiral decoration. It is supposed that the distinctive Minoan figure eight oxhide shields, which protected the whole body, hung on the north wall. The floors were paved with gypsum flags. Other polythyra on the east and south side led into a wide portico with square pillar in the corner and beyond this there may have been an open terrace overlooking the valley of the river Kairatos.

A narrow passage leads from the Hall of the Double Axes to the so-called Queen's Megaron (ill. 35, 37). Some of the windows on the south and east side of which open onto two light-wells and the benches beneath them have been restored. The wall-paintings here are of considerable importance and include the Dolphin fresco (ill. 32) which depicts these intelligent creatures frolicking in the sea, surrounded by flying fish. The dolphins are deep blue with white bellies and a yellow band along their sides. Certain details of this fresco, such as the sea spray, are quite remarkable. A border of coral frames the entire composition. At a later date another wall-painting of spirals covered the first. The originals are, of course, in the Herakleion Museum (ill. 33) along with that of the charming dancing girl with long, billowing tresses (ill.34). In this room different phases of floor construction can be discerned. A narrow flight of steps leads to the upper storey which may have been the original home of the Dolphin Fresco, for it possibly adorned a shrine dedicated to the goddess of the sea. West of the "Megaron" is a small room thought to have been a bathroom (ill. 36), though the clay bath tub, of the same type as used as coffins, may not actually have stood where we see it today. According to a more recent and plausible interpretation this was infact a bed chamber. A dark corridor decorated with spiral frescoes leads from the "Queen's Megaron" to the "Queen's Dressing Room", as it has been called, and to the lavatory which would have had a wooden seat and was connected up with the palace's elaborate plumbing system. The entire installation is remarkable for the time, but the Minoans' love of cleanliness is renowned. Beyond is a light-well known as the Court of the Distaffs because the sign of the distaff (if indeed this is what is represented) is incised on its walls. In a nearby room, a kind of treasury, diverse precious objects were discovered, including a tiny gold fish. Further on a service staircase leads to the upper floor where there are several restored rooms.

The southern sector of the East Wing also contains several interesting places. In one room with a low plaster partition a clay bathtub is still preserved. Actually inside this partition a number of vases decorated with white lilies were found. The whole suite of rooms, which is associated with an adjacent lustral basin, perhaps belonged to a priest. After the 1600 BC destruction the apartment was completely filled in and served as a base for a new one which was built upon it. Of especial interest is the square Shrine of the Double Axes to the south (ill. 38) which was converted into a shrine in Postpalatial times. The room is divided into three sections, each at a different level. In the northernmost there is a pebbled bench on which diverse cult objects were arrayed, such as two pairs of plaster sacral horns with small holes in the centre for affixing double axes or small branches. The shrine was thus named after a small steatite double axe with double-honed edges found there. Various clay figurines were also found on this ledge, one representing the familiar Minoan goddess with arms raised in a gesture of blessing and a dove perched symbolically on her head (ill. 62). Her bell-shaped skirt is reminiscent of a crinoline. This type of figurine was common in later Minoan times. Several vases and a tripod altar were found in front of this ledge. West of the Shrine of the Double Axes is a corridor in which clay Linear B tablets, in the Greek language but with Minoan characters, (ill. 65) were brought to light.

Beyond this complex of rooms, which has another light-well, a lustral basin and a flight of stairs, and which delineates the southeast corner of the palace there are several private houses constituting part of the town. The closest, nowadays roofed with cement, has been called the House of the Chancel Screen. It has a lustral basin, three magazines and a crypt with a square pillar in the middle. In the centre of the building is a spacious hall with polythyra (pier and door partitions). Next to it is the so-called South-east House and close to this a kiln. West of the first house are two smaller ones, the House of the Sacrificed Oxen and the House of the Fallen blocks, separated by a paved street. The first house, with an L-shaped room, perhaps belonged to a stone-cutter. The other, with four rooms, was named after several huge blocks which had fallen from a wall of the palace and had destroyed it. The weight of some of these blocks, in excess of a ton, indicates the terrific intensity of the earthquake.

Returning to the royal quarters, we pass along a long corridor which divides the east wing into two and so enter its north sector which housed the palace workshops. In this corridor too numerous Linear B tablets were found.

A portal at its east end leads into the Lobby of the Wooden Posts, so named after the beams used to reinforce the walls, imparting resilience as an anti-seismic precaution in accordance with the usual method in Minoan architecture. Next to it is the Eastern Portico with four columns and a staircase to the south. It was built after the destruction of 1500 BC. West of this portico is the Lapidary's Workshop in which unworked blocks of basalt ("lapis Lacedaemonius") were found, imported from a Spartan quarry and used for the manufacture of high quality stone vases. Some of these blocks bear traces of working, which was suddenly interrupted by the destruction of the palace. The main workshops were probably in the upper storey, the provenance of a number of half-finished stone vases. The room to the north is known as the Schoolroom on account of the benches around three of its walls with stone basins beside them. It has been interpreted either as a school for apprentice scribes, or as an atelier of student painters or potters. It was re-used during the "reoccupation" period. The "Schoolroom" is linked with the so-called Court of the Stone Spout, named after the end of a drainage pipe, visible high up on the west wall, which conveyed water from the light-well into a small cistern which was connected to a well. In the southwest corner of the court the famous Toreador Fresco, which vividly portrays the dangerous sport of bull-leaping in which girls clad in male clothing also participated (ill. 95), hangs. Along the side of the Central Court runs the Corridor of the Bays, a conventional name given on account of its three blind magazines. At the far end was a doorway. Various interesting objects were found in nearby rooms, such as Kamares vases, clay models of royal palanquins and, last but not least, the well-known "Town Mosaic", a series of faience plaques depicting the facades of houses, an invaluable source of information on hitherto unknown details of Minoan architecture. Adjacent to the Corridor of the Bays is the long magazine of the Medallion Pithoi in which some of these enormous storage jars with relief medallion decoration are still "in situ". Nearby the wall-painting of the elegant Minoan "Ladies in blue" was revealed (ill. 96). In one small room were perhaps the remains of a colossal statue of the Goddess, apparently some three metres high and mainly of wood, like the Archaic xoana, as perhaps indicated by the charred heap, which had fallen from the upper storey together with three bronze locks of hair which were perhaps originally gilded. These remains are the sole - and uncertain- testimony of the existence of large statues in the Minoan era, though they were certainly not numerous.

The East Bastion forms the east entrance to the palace, low down and facing the Kairatos valley. It has the appearance of a bastion with flights of stairs inside, but is not infact a fortification work despite its name. Alongside each flight of steps runs a steep, open conduit for rain water, the bottom of which describes a parabolic curve to break the force of water flow by creating a succession of small waterfalls to avoid splashing. The ingenuity of the constructor is indeed impressive. There are small settling tanks at intervals to filter out the sediment and it was believed initially that the area below the East Bastion was the palace laundry. According to another viewpoint the arena for bull-sports was located here.

Mounting a large staircase leading to the Central Court, we observe on our right the Magazines of the Giant Pithoi, part of the storerooms of the East Wing of the Early palace. These pithoi have several handles and bear relief decoration imitating the rope tied around their body for reinforcement. The gigantic proportions of these pithoi brings to mind the myth of Glaukos, son of Minos, who fell into just such a jar full of honey and was drowned. There are other Early palace magazines to the north, in which Kamares style vases were found, while to the west is the Corridor of the Draughtboard, so named after the famous royal gaming board brought to light there. This game, from the end of the Middle Minoan period, somewhat reminiscent of chess, was made of gilded ivory inset with squares of rock crystal and faience. Close by four large conical pawns of ivory were found, possibly used as dice. Under the floor of this corridor part of the complex plumbing system of the palace can be seen, indeed remarkable for those early times.

From the north of the Central Court a long, narrow corridor, the North Entrance passage (ill. 40) leads to the north entrance to the palace. This was an unroofed, paved passage with a steep downward gradient. Some time later two structures resembling bastions were erected on either side, considerably reducing its width. Porticoes were built on top of these "bastions" at the same height as the Court. The West Portico has been restored and is accessible via a small stairway. A copy of the enormous relief fresco of a charging bull, of the end of the Middle Minoan period, has been placed in its original position (ill.

41). It has been supposed that the scene represented a bull-fight or the capture of a wild bull in nets, a subject also illustrated in relief on the renowned gold cups from Vapheio near Sparta, which are generally regarded as being of Minoan workmanship. The fierce creature is rendered in a most convincing manner and beside it is an olive tree with colourful foliage. Part of a human figure can be discerned on one fresco fragment. A similar wall-painting perhaps embellished the other bastion. This enormous picture of a bull, which is thought to have survived into later Greek times, may, it is said, have played a role in the formulation of the legend of the Minotaur.

The North Entrance Passage leads through a doorway with adjacent porter's lodge, into a spacious hypostyle hall with two rows of eight square pillars and two terminal columns. This hall has been rather fancifully named the Customs House, since it was next to the sea gate of the palace (ill. 42). In actual fact it was probably a banqueting hall with another room above. There is a gateway on the west side of the "Customs House".

In the southwest corner of the Central Court and to the west of the North Entrance passage stands a rectangular structure with very deep foundations and rounded corners, a remnant of the Early Palace. It has been named the North Keep and is considered to have been one of the insulae, the independent architectural units which, according to Evans, formed the first palace. Inside there are six very deep, narrow rooms, probably magazines, known as the "cells" or "dungeons", which were subsequently filled in with earth. A shrine with paved floor and central pillar was erected on top. The walls of one of the rooms in the new structure were decorated with two well-known miniature paintings, the "Sacred Grove" and the "Tripartite Shrine". In a nearby room the "Saffron Gatherer fresco" a monkey in a meadow of crocuses was found. Since the head of the animal was missing, it was initially thought to depict a young boy.

Outside the palace, at a short distance from the gateway of the "Customs House" is a restored North Lustral Basin (ill. 44) with a staircase with stepped parapet and columns. There was a gypsum dado around its walls and above these were frescoes imitating sponge impressions. Beyond, to the northwest, lies the "Theatral Area" of Knossos (ill. 43), a rectangular paved space with tiers of seats along two sides and a bastion-like structure at their junction, a kind of "Royal Box". Perhaps from here the royal family and some 500 seated spectators watched such spectacles as religious ceremonies or even wrestling or boxing bouts. A conduit alongside the seats was for collecting rainwater. This "Theatre" maybe copies the earlier corresponding structure at the palace of Phaistos . It is from the "Theatral Area" that the well-paved "Royal Road" (ill. 45), the "oldest road in Europe", commences. On either side there are private houses, such as the "Arsenal", in which tablets recording a large number of arrows were found, and the "House of the Frescoes" with scenes of plants, monkeys and birds.

The Royal Road leads directly to the main road north of the palace and the famous Little palace. A columned propylon forms the main entrance and a paved peristyle court extends in front of the main hall of the building, connected with it by a polythyron. An identical pdythyron divides the hall into two. During the final phase of the building's habitation a lustral basin to the west was converted into a shrine in which sacral horns and four pieces of stalagmite, vaguely resembling human forms, were found. In the southwest corner of the building there was a lavatory installation connected to a drain outside. A gypsum staircase next to the court led to the upper storey. In the south sector of the building there was a basement with two crypts containing square pillars. The most important find from the Little Palace is the splendid bull's-head rhyton (ill. 87), a libation vessel of black steatite which originally had gilded wooden horns. Only one of the eyes was preserved, of rock crystal painted on the underside. This vessel ranks among the masterpieces of Minoan art.

# HERAKLEION MUSEUM

The Herakleion Museum is the second largest Greek museum but unique in importance since, as the central museum of Crete, it represents almost exclusively the Minoan civilization, the oldest civilization developed on European soil. In most of the twenty rooms and galleries of the museum are exhibited in chronological order the movable remains of this great civilization, which extends over almost the whole of the third and second millennia B.C. From the treasures of the museum is here presented a selection of the most representative objects of the art of Prehistoric Crete.

Pottery, the most important feature and the most basic form of artistic expression of every ancient civilization — and especially of a prehistoric one — the first element for determining chronology. According to the system of Arthur Evans, the Bronze Age which succeeded the very long Neolithic or New Stone Age a little after the beginning of the third millennium B.C. is divided in three periods, Early Minoan (EM), Middle Minoan (MM) and Late Minoan (LM), and each of these into three sub-periods. Nicholas Platon applied alternatively another triadic system according to the history of the palaces. Thus he divides the Bronze Age into Prepalatial, Protopalatial or period of the First or Early Palaces, since about 2000 B.C., Neopalatial or period of the Later Palaces, since about 1700 B.C., and Postpalatial, after the final destruction of Knossos in about 1375 B.C. or a little later.

The so-called Pyrgos Ware belongs to the EM I phase. It was named after a location near Knossos but has been found in several other places all over Crete. In plate 46 we see the most common shape of the Pyrgos Ware, a sort of chalice on a very high and almost conical pedestal. It has been assumed that this shape perhaps imitates a wooden original. The surface of the vessels is black to grey. The burnished decoration is hardly distinguishable on the matt surface.

To the same early phase belong the vases of the Hagios Onouphrios Ware, named after a place near Phaistos where such pottery was found for the first time ill. 47. Decoration is linear, red or brown on a light background. It usually resembles a net. This ware, which perhaps originates from Asia Minor, is richly represented in the Mesara Plain, in south Central Crete. The jug in the picture rests on three small feet.

Another Prepalatial ware, which is dated to the next period (EM II), is the well-known Vasiliki Ware. Such pottery was found for the first time in the archaeological site of Vasiliki on the Isthmus of Hierapetra, in Eastern Crete, but was popular over almost the whole island. A characteristic shape is the tall beak-spouted jug in plate 5 4, Vasiliki Ware pottery is hand-made but so shapely as to appear to have been made by means of the potter's wheel, which however had not yet been invented. The surface of the vessel displays a mottled red-brown and black decoration, which is very attractive. This decoration was obviously obtained by means of uneven firing of the surface, of course accidental at first but later deliberate. Perhaps they applied a burning twig to different parts of the vase.

A quite different class are the stone vases, indeed an achievement of Minoan art. Those we see in plate 5 3 come from the Early Minoan cemetery on the small island of Mochlos, in Eastern Crete. One of them looks like a teapot with a long horizontal spout. Contemporary is the pyxis (box) of schist in figure 5 1 found inside a small tomb near Maronia, Siteia. The cover is decorated with spirals in relief. The vessel shows a pronounced Cycladic influence or is perhaps imported from the Cyclades, which had developed a remarkable civilization during these early times. Stone vases were manufactured throughout the entire Bronze Age, from as early as the EM II period, but the first ones were imported to Crete as becomes clear also from their developed shapes. Their manufacture required essentially the use of a drill rotated at high speed. In the beginning they employed soft stones only. The artist always exploited the veins and colours of the various stones to the best advantage. The vessels display a great variety of shapes and sizes. Some are miniature and others quite large. Most of them seem never to have been used for practical purposes since only a few were found in settlements.

The art of Early Minoan Crete is also famous for its jewellery. The treasure in plate 5 2 also comes from the cemetery of Mochlos. These elegant jewels, made of gold foil, imitate sprays of leaves and daisies, put on hairpins. These tombs yielded jewels of various types. Most important are the diadems. This early jewellery is inspired by the most ancient art of Mesopotamia, from jewels found inside the Royal Tombs of the Sumerians at Ur.

With the emergence of the palaces and the entry of Crete into a higher degree of civilization at the beginning of the Middle Minoan period, pottery reached an unsurpassable artistic quality. Kamares Ware, named after the sacred cave of Kamares on Mount Ida, the modern Psiloritis, where it was first found, is perhaps the most beautiful prehistoric style. The polychrome decoration is rich in imagination and full of movement, dynamism and delicacy. Well-known is a beak-spouted jug from the early palace at Phaistos (pl 57), perfectly preserved, with spiral and leaf-like motifs on a black ground. From the same palace comes the large fruitstand of (ill.55), covered with abstract motifs, as well as the krater of (ill.56), on a high pedestal, adorned with large flowers in relief, perhaps lilies. This vase, which reaches twenty inches (fifty centimetres) in height, surely imitates one of stone and metal. Kamares Ware is intimately related to the palace workshops.

Undoubtedly the most splendid Minoan jewel is the bee pendant from Malia which was also found inside a tomb, a large sepulchral building characteristically known as Chrysolakkos (the "Gold Hole") after the treasure found here. This jewel is dated to the seventeenth century B.C.(ill.60) heraldically confronted bees frame a small disk which represents the honeycomb and is decorated with tiny granulation. Above the insects' heads is a sort of small cage with a gold bead inside. From the jewel hang three disks.

Some of the weapons of the Minoans, which belonged to a leader or were employed during some important ceremony, were real masterpieces. Several splendid swords were recovered from the early palace of Malia. The sword in (ill.1) had a wooden hilt covered with gold foil and, below it, a gold disk with the representation of a youth bending his body backwards forming a circle, with the feet touching the head. These swords were very long, reaching forty inches (one metre). They were made not for cutting but only for thrusting. Many votive swords were found in the well-known sacred cave at Arkalochori.

Also from the palace of Malia comes the royal axe of (ill.61), made of schist. This object, perhaps the head of a sceptre, on one side ended in a battle-axe and the other in the form of an attacking panther. The surface is adorned with spirals in a tight arrangement. This splendid work was made during the second half of the sixteenth century.

Some of the best works of Minoan art, products of the palace workshops, are made of faience. They were manufactured by means of moulds. The largest collection of faience artifacts was recovered from the so-called Temple Repositories, in the west wing of the palace at Knossos, datable to the peak of the Minoan civilization, round about 1600 B.C. Among them are the appliqué reliefs of an antelope with her offspring and of a cow suckling her calf (fig. 59), small masterpieces which express perfectly the naturalism of this art. Quite famous are the polychrome Snake Goddesses, from the same place; these statuettes display the elegance of the garments of the Minoan woman (pl. 62). The tallest goddess, to the left, measuring 14 inches (34 centimetres), has her large white breasts bare. She wears a tall tiara on the head with a snake coiled around it. Other snakes are coiled around her body. The smaller goddess is similarly dressed. Her posture is slightly different. There is a small cat or leopard on top of a cap on her head. Both goddesses wear long skirts.

It is not known whether these figures represent goddesses or priestesses. In any case, whatever the artist's intention, these statuettes, together with other archaeological evidence, reveal the great cultic significance of the snake in Minoan religion, which symbolized eternity and immortality. These beliefs of the Minoans were inherited by Classical Greece, where the house snake was considered as a beneficial spirit. On the other hand, the goddess Athena, with her sacred snake on the Acropolis, is in a way the successor of the Minoan Snake Goddess.

Equally famous but surely much more mysterious is the Phaistos Disk (pl. 58). This solid clay disk, with a diameter of sixteen centimetres, found at the beginning of this century in the excavations of Phaistos together with objects datable around 1600 B.C., is covered on both sides with an unknown ideographic script with 241 characters. The inscription takes the shape of a spiral and goes from the circumference to the centre. Some archaeologists believe that the disk was not made in Crete. Each character of the inscription was impressed into the wet clay by means of a stamp, perhaps of metal. This is indeed a very ancient precursor of printing. Among these signs, which are like pictures (pictographic), we see figures representing men, women and children, vases, animals, fish, birds, insects, ships and others. The text of the inscription has not yet been actually deciphered, despite the labour of many scholars. The bibliography about it is huge. The text must be rather a religious hymn, perhaps incantations with a magical meaning, or an astrological chart.

If archaeology has not yet been able to decipher the Phaistos Disk, this is not the case with the Linear B script, which is written on oblong clay tablets (fig. 65). This script replaced the so-called Linear A, which is supposed to represent the Minoan language, while the Linear B renders Mycenaean Greek. It is almost exclusively found in Knossos, after the great destruction of 1450 B.C. and the installation of Achaian rulers in the palace. These tablets, which seem to have been simple accounting notes of the economic administration of the palace, contain numbers and lists, things difficult to remember, and are written in a syllabic system, though some signs are ideographic. Tablets are usually found in palatial archives, but their preservation is due to chance, to a fire which destroyed the building and baked the clay which was originally sun-dried. The writing was done from left to right.

One of the most beautiful materials used by the Minoan artists was ivory. They had made seals and amulets ever since Early Minoan times. Later, the palace workshops manufactured small ivory statuettes, real masterpieces like the well-known acrobat from Knossos, of the sixteenth century B.C.(ill.68). This lean and well-formed figure surely represents a naked youth engaged in bull-leaping, at the moment of execution of this difficult and dangerous sport. The bull has completely disappeared. The acrobat is much restored. The details of the body, like the veins of the hands and the fingernails, are very interesting. Several minute holes in the head indicate that it was originally covered with hair, perhaps of gold. There are also other chryselephantine statuettes, made in separate pieces which were assembled at the end.

Ivory was imported — probably from Syria — unworked in the form of elephant tusks, as has been proved in the excavations of the palace of Zakros, where some complete tusks were found, blackened by fire. From sections of such tusks, cylindrical boxes were often manufactured, with fine decoration in relief. Such a box was found recently inside a tomb at Katsambas, the harbour-town of Knossos (ill. 2). The elaborate decoration illustrates, in a naturalistic way, the hunting and capture of a wild bull by three men in a rocky landscape. There is also a palm-tree. This is a subject popular in Minoan art, seen also on the famous contemporary cups from Vapheio, which are considered to be of Cretan manufacture. The box is a work of the fifteenth century B.C. The vivid movement of the scenes is characteristic. Perhaps it is dealing with bulls destined for the bull-games.

A small plaque from Palaikastro, of the same material, illustrates an imaginary bird flying among stylized rocks and clouds (ill. 77). The scene was continued in a row of similar plaques.

A relief "sacred knot" is also made of ivory, of Middle Minoan date, from Knossos (ill. 67). The sacred knot, as this ceremonial symbol of the Minoan religion has been named, which is often combined with the double axe, surely had a magical meaning. The Egyptian goddess Isis had a knot corresponding to the Minoan one. Similar symbols are known from later times, such as the well-known Gordian Knot, which was connected with the history of Alexander the Great.

The double axe is undoubtedly the most important and representative symbol of the Minoan religion and her goddess, as well as the most common tool of the time. The ceremonial axes, which of course were not intended for actual use, were made of various materials such as bronze, gold and silver, in various sizes, from the huge to the miniature. Such ceremonial or votive axes are recovered from excavations of sacred places. A great number comes from the sacred cave near Arkalochori (ill. 50). The double axe is interpreted as a special symbol of the Great Mother Goddess. The famous labyrinth has been considered as the dwelling of the "labrys", the double axe. This very ancient symbol, which originates in the Orient, appears also on seals which surely are of an amuletic nature, as well as on clay coffins and vessels of ceremonial importance. Such a vase, a work of 1500 B.C., in the form of a basket, comes from Pseira, a small island in the Gulf of Mirabello with an important Minoan settlement, settlement (ill. 69). The axe appears in four superimposed rows, in a dense arrangement.

The religious beliefs of the Minoans are still quite unknown to us, since we cannot read their cult texts and we have to rely on analogies and parallels with other ancient religions, or what survived in the later Greek worship. We gain a glimpse into this lost world through the miniature religious scenes illustrated on the Minoan gold finger-rings. These rings were in fact not worn on the finger, because their diameter is too small, but they had a sphragistic use and were perhaps hung around the neck. A splendid example of miniature art is the finger-ring of Late Minoan times found inside the large tholos tomb at Isopata, near Knossos (ill.48). The scene shows women in long garments dancing a ceremonial dance in a meadow strewn with flowers. A diminutive figure in the upper left corner has been considered to represent the divinity appearing in response to the invocation of the women.

Another religious practice, strange for modern conceptions but also known from other parts of the world, was swinging: in a clay model from Hagia Triada, fifteen centimetres high, we see a swinging woman, while doves sit on top of the posts of the swing, characteristic symbols of the divine presence, the epiphany of the goddess (ill. 63).

Still another aspect of Minoan religion is connected with the cycle of the worship of the dead. A unique clay model has been found inside a tholos tomb near the village of Kamilaris, in the Mesara Plain (fig.75).This construction, with two columns in the foreground, is rectangular. In the background sit four dead persons, each behind an altar or table, while two living ones, in a smaller scale stand before the altars and offer them food and drink.

The naturalism of Minoan art reaches its peak in the vase-painting of the beginning of the Late Minoan period, though a certain stylization is not absent. The so-called Floral Style covers the LM IA phase (about 1550-1500 B.C.). The graceful floral motifs stem from frescoes. They are made with black paint on a yellowish background. The "jug of the reeds" from the second palace of Phaistos is splendid (pl.72). The reed-like plants cover the whole vase in a dense arrangement and adapt themselves to its form. In the next phase, the LM IB (about 1500-1450 B.C.), the Marine Style was created, perhaps in the palace workshops of Knossos. A variety of marine creatures appear round the vessel in a perfectly life-like way, as if swimming. From Eastern Crete, again from Palaikastro, comes a flask-like vessel, with an octopus with large eyes and waving tentacles (pl. 76). There is a background of seaweed. Similar is a stirrup-jar from Gournia, a very popular vessel form, mainly during the last centuries of the Bronze Age. These exquisite Marine Style vases, the best of their period, were exported to other countries. Later, these naturalistic motifs lost their freshness and became stylized.

Perhaps the most characteristic artifacts of the Minoan civilization are seals. They appear in Crete for the first time as early as the EM II period. Of course their origin is from the Orient, but in Crete they acquired a totally new spirit and originality. Their manufacture soon transcended their practical usefulness and evolved into a real art. In the beginning they employed soft materials like ivory, bone and various not hard stones. Most subjects on the early seals are decorative and abstract, sometimes quite complex. A large ivory seal coming from a Prepalatial tomb of the Mesara Plain (fig. 3) until now unpublished, shows an interesting composition, a whirling motif. Later, an improved technique allowed the use even of hard stones. Some seals were of metal or clay. The most usual seals are amygdaloid (almond-shaped) or lentoid (lens-shaped), like the two in plates 73 and 74 found inside tombs at Knossos, of the fifteenth century, the era of the acme of gem-cutting. Only one of the two convex sides was engraved. Such seals could be worn around the wrist, as we see on the frescoes, or around the neck.

The former of these seals (pl. 73) illustrates a lion devouring a galloping bull. Such scenes are quite common in the repertoire of seal-engraving and express the love of the artist for subjects taken from nature and full of movement. The posture of the animals adapts itself perfectly to the round field of the seal. Perhaps the scene had also some religious symbolism. The lion, despite its mane, is characteristically female.

The latter seal (pl. 74) represents a clearly religious scene: the goddess stands at the centre with upraised arms, flanked by two winged griffins, sacred monsters which play the role of followers of the divinities and guardians of the sacred places. Above the head of the goddess the double axe can be distinguished. Many seals had no practical use but were magical amulets which protected the person wearing them.

Minoan sculpture does not express itself by means of large statues, as was the rule in other countries and times. On the contrary, the Cretan artist preferred small figurines of clay and statuettes of bronze and other materials. Very characteristic is the bronze worshipper from Tylissos, in a posture of attention (pl. 49). The right hand is raised ceremonially to the brow, almost like a military salute. The surface of the bronze has been left intentionally rough and looks like an impressionistic work of modern times. The statuette is datable to the LM I period. It is solid and was cast in the then customary method of "cire perdue" (lost wax), a model of wax which was covered with clay and afterwards was used as a mould.

The sculptor does not express himself only through sculpture in the round but also through works in relief. Famous are the three stone vases from the villa at Hagia Triada, of the second half of the sixteenth century B.C., realistic works of the time of the zenith of the palatial civilization.

The Boxer Vase, made of serpentine, is conical and high (pl. 81). Several parts have been adroitly restored. The surface is divided into four zones, with vivid scenes of boxing. The bodies of the boxers are very athletic and muscular. Most of them wear heavy bronze helmets. This sport, which must have had a long tradition, perhaps had some religious meaning. On one of the zones of the vessel is the representation of a bull-fight, or rather a bull-game, executed in a very realistic way, with the athlete passing above the head of the huge animal.

The second vase is the so-called Chieftain Cup (pl. 79). On it is illustrated a young man with long hair holding a staff or sceptre reaching to the ground, some important person, a chieftain. Before him stands an officer holding a sword and a lustral sprinkler. Three men come behind the officer carrying large hides, as they have been interpreted, perhaps for the manufacture of shields. They are perhaps the hides of sacrificed bulls.

The third vessel is the so-called Harvester Vase, made also of serpentine (pl. 80). Its shape looks like an ostrich's egg. The shoulders are covered with a life-like rustic scene of a group of peasants who advance laughing and singing. They are headed by an elderly man holding a stick, who wears a strange ceremonial cloak. Four of the peasants sing, forming a real quartet, while one of them holds an object resembling an Egyptian sistrum.

During recent years another libation rhyton has been added to the known masterpieces, found in the palace of Zakros (pl. 82). Its surface was gilded, as shown by some traces which have survived. A typical Minoan tripartite shrine is illustrated, with its central section higher than the other two on the sides. In front of it are altars. On the roof of the shrine Cretan ibexes sit facing one another while others run around and birds fly. The landscape is rocky and the scene has been considered as representing a peak sanctuary, one of those important places of worship and pilgrimage of the Minoans on the peaks of the mountains, which were in the open air but often had also a small shrine. The pilgrims brought here small votive figurines, which today are found in great numbers in the excavations. The figurines represent humans and animals, whole herds in miniature. The human figurines, men and women with elegant garments and fantastically elaborate coiffures, surely represent the pilgrims themselves. In (ill. 85)are two figurines from the great sanctuary at Petsophas, on the eastern coast of Crete. The male figurine, naked excepting the peculiar Minoan loincloth, has a long dagger obliquely stuck in his belt. The female figurine features a characteristic high collar which became fashionable again at the time of the European Renaissance. The skirt has white designs on a black ground. Both figurines make ceremonial gestures. Quite interesting is the custom of offering votive human limbs in the hope of invoking the blessing of the divinity and the cure of an illness.

An astounding collection of stone vases was found in the palace of Zakros. Remarkable among them are an amphora of veined marble with high spiral handles (pl. 83) and a tall chalice of spotted obsidian for the sacred communion (pl. 84). The existence of this ceremony where these special chalices were employed was known from representations on frescoes and seals, but at Zakros actual examples were found for the first time. The composition of the holy liquid is not known.

To the family of the stone vases belongs also the plastic rhyton of black steatite in the shape of a bull's head from Knossos (pl. 87) found inside a well of the Little Palace. The original horns of the bull, made of wood covered with gold foil, did not survive but were reconstructed according to a summary sketch of the head found incised on the rhyton's base. Only one of the eyes of the animal is still in situ, made of rock crystal painted red and black on the underside. Round the nostrils is white shell inlay. The holy liquid inside the rhyton was perhaps the blood of the sacrificed bull itself, as some archaeologists presume.

The pottery of the Palace Style, thus named because it is found mainly at the palace of Knossos, flourished during the LM II period, about 1450-1400 B.C. A remarkable example of this style is the pithos of plate 86, which has large double axes with decorated surfaces, rosettes and stylized plants. This style has a monumental character but at the same time is rather conventional and without much originality and life. The naturalistic motifs of the earlier styles, Floral and Marine, are still used but in a formalistic way. The Palace Style is rather foreign to the Cretan spirit and it seems that it was imported to Knossos by the Achaian rulers.

The original libation jug of plate 88, found inside a tomb at Katsambas, is dated to just before the end of the Neopalatial period. The elegant shape of the vessel is pronounced through the long spout and the rows of vertical thorn-like projections. On the surface are painted nautili and inversed papyrus flowers, very stylized.

The extremely long Postpalatial LM III period (about 1400-1100 B.C.) is the last one of the Bronze Age. The palaces lay in ruins but Crete was a wealthy part of the Mycenaean world. Art continued to be noteworthy, more Minoan than Mycenaean. The dead were buried in clay coffins ("larnakes"), which either have the shape of a bathtub, or are rectangular on short thick legs with a gabled lid, which imitate in a coarse clay a wooden original, a house chest. Typical is the chest-like larnax of plate 71 from Vasilika Anogeia in Central Crete, datable round about 1350 B.C. The surface is painted with motifs of this time, like those used in vase-painting, stylized water-fowl, papyrus flowers and fish. These coffins are too short for an outstretched body but it seems that the dead, who returned to the Mother Earth, were given the posture of an embryo. Other coffins are decorated with octopuses with very long tentacles, often less than eight, palm-trees which surely had a cultic meaning, as well as various holy symbols.

Late Minoan sculpture expresses itself mainly through small hand-made clay figurines. A group from Palaikastro represents three women dancing with outstretched arms forming the section of a circle round another woman playing the lyre (pl. 78). This vivid scene has been considered as perhaps representing the dance of Classical Crete known as h y p o r c h e m a. At the end of the period appeared a type of female statuette, the so-called Household Goddess or Goddess with upraised arms, in a characteristic posture of blessing. The torso of the statuette rests on a cylindrical wheel-made base, forming a sort of crinoline. Well-known is the so-called Goddess of the Poppies from Gazi near Herakleion, 2 feet 6 inches or 75 centimetres high (pl. 89). Three opium poppy-heads sprout

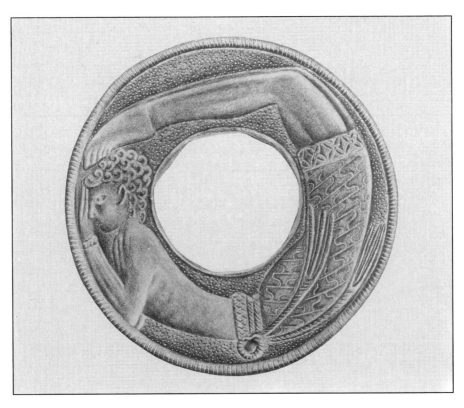

1. *Acrobat of gold foil from a ceremonial sword.*
  *Palace of Malia.*

from her diadem. These flowers surely had a religious significance and perhaps denote the ecstatic nature of Minoan worship. In the same place another goddess was found, a little smaller, with pairs of sacral horns and birds on her head.

The helmets made of boars' tusks, described by Homer, are famous. A helmet of this kind was found inside a tomb at Zafer Papoura, near Knossos, and is dated to the beginning of the LM III period, a little before the final destruction of the palace. The helmet was placed at the feet of the warrior (pl. 70). The tusks were fastened on a leather cap in horizontal rows, with alternating direction in each row. These helmets possibly have their origin in the trophies of the hunt.

From Hagia Triada comes the votive clay model of a ship in figure 4, dated to LM III times. The mast, the sail, the halyards and the rest of the attachments of the vessel are of course a modern conjectural restoration. Much discussed among specialists is the problem whether the higher end, seen on many pictures of Minoan vessels, often on sealstones, is the prow or the stern.

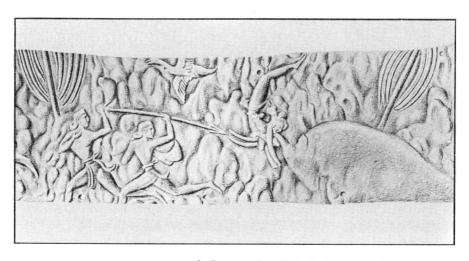

*2. Capture of a wild bull. Ivory pyxis from Katsambas.*
*(Drawing by Thomas Phanourakis).*

The upper floor of the Herakleion Museum houses the remains of Minoan painting. A unique monument is the sarcophagus from Hagia Triada (pls 90-92, a work of 1400 B.C. It is made of limestone and was found without a cover. On four sides are scenes of a religious character of utmost importance for the evidence they give about the rather mysterious Minoan religion, its ceremonies and the after-life beliefs of the Prehistoric Cretans. On one side (pl. 90), to the left, two women pour libations into a vessel set among two huge double axes. Birds are perched on them, symbolizing the presence of the divinity. The offering of the liquid is made to the music of a lyre. To the right of the picture appears the dead man himself in front of the door of his tomb, clad in a long garment which conceals his arms. Like the ghost of Patroclus in the Iliad, the dead man starts to sink below the surface of the earth. Three men in strange garments come in front of him, bringing two calves and a model boat, perhaps for the voyage to the Land of the Dead. The other side of the sarcophagus (pl. 91) illustrates, among others, the sacrifice of a bull, bound on a special sacrificial table. Each narrow side has a chariot with two goddesses. One chariot is drawn by winged griffins (pl. 92).

A purely palatial art was the painting of the frescoes. The colours were made from mineral materials. The pictures, true frescoes, were painted on the

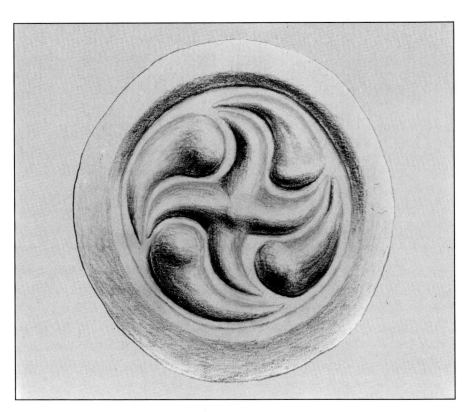

*3. Pre-palatial ivory seal from tholos tomb B, Apesokari.
(Drawing by Thomas Phanourakis).*

wet plaster by skilful and quick artists, sometimes on a guiding sketch. Some figures were moulded in slight relief. According to the Egyptian model, male figures were painted in dark colours and female ones in white. Later, the painting of Classical Greece followed this model.

The Minoan wall-paintings illustrate nature, court life and the religious ceremonies. Their subjects are not historical or monumental. Figures are shown in profile, like in Egypt. Landscapes are rendered in a conventional way. This art of the Minoans, extremely vivid and attractive, disappeared together with the palaces.

Surely the most famous fresco from the palace of Knossos is the girl known as the "Parisienne" (pl. 93), as she was named by the workers of the excavation.

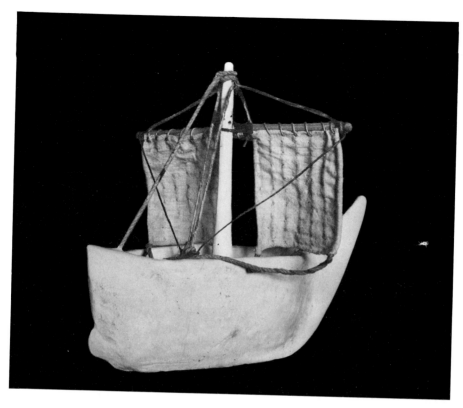

*4. Post-palatial clay replica of a boat from Hagia Triada, partially restored.*

She is probably a goddess, but perhaps also a priestess. On her back we see a large sacral knot. The coiffure is elaborate, the eyes huge, the mouth scarlet. This figure is part of a larger wall-painting in two zones.

Another well-known figure is the majestic "Prince of the Lilies" or the "Priest-King" (pl. 94). This relief-fresco is much restored, even the face. The diadem of the youthful prince has lilies and three long peacock's plumes falling behind. The prince perhaps leads a sacred monster, possibly a sphinx.

Another Knossian fresco, also much restored, is the "Ladies in blue" (pl. 96). These court ladies, with their wonderful hair-does and rich garments which leave the breasts bare, show all the elegance and joy of the Minoan society. The ladies perhaps assist at some spectacle.

31

Very instructive about the way of performing the bull-games is the well-known fresco from the east wing of Knossos (pl. 95). Of course, we cannot speak about bull-fights but rather about bull-games, as the athletes did not use any weapons to kill the bull. In the picture we see a girl in the typical male attire grasping the horns of a huge bull charging in gallop. A young man has already turned a somersault over the animal's head, while another girl with outstretched arms, behind the bull, stands by to help him. These difficult and dangerous sports had possibly a religious meaning.

Not all Minoan wall-paintings were of such large dimensions as those we have already seen. Some of them illustrate scenes in a very small scale. Very interesting is the "Palace Feast" (pl. 97), a miniature fresco thus named because we are able to recognize the Tripartite Shrine of the palace of Knossos, in the middle of the west side of the Central Court. The crowd is composed mainly of men, who are conventionally rendered in a brown sun-burned colour, in contrast to the women who are white.

5. Knossos. Topography of the area (plan C. Iliakis).
1. The Palace
2. The «Little Palace»
3. «Caravan Serai»
4. «Royal Villa»
5. «House of the Frescoes»
6. Minoan road
7. «Arsenal»
8. «Customs house»
9. Northeast house
10. Minoan houses
11. Minoan quarry
12. Minoan bridge
13. «Stepped portico»
14. River Kairatos
15. Gypsades hill
16. Modern village of Makrytoichos

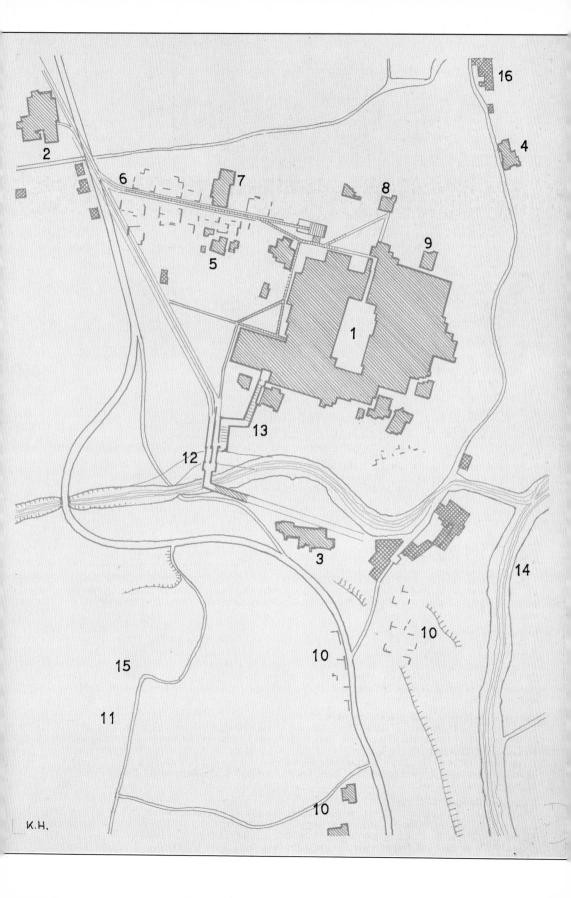

K.H.

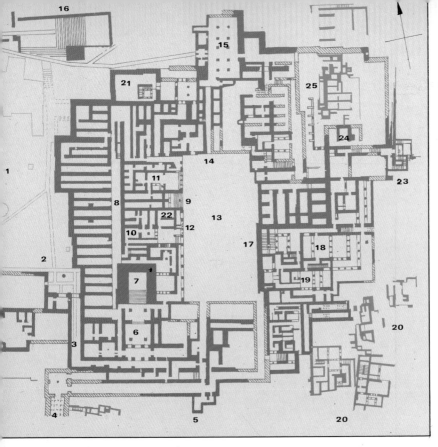

7. Γενική άποψη τ
ανακτόρου της Κνωσ

General vi
of the palace of Knoss

Vue génér
du palais de Cnoss

Gesamtansi
des Palastes von Knoss

Veduta gener
del Palazzo di Cnos

**6. Ανάκτορο της Κνωσού. (Σχ. Κ. Ηλιάκη).**
*1. Δυτική Αυλή. 2. Δυτικό Πρόπυλο. 3. Διάδρομος της Πομπής. 4. Βαθμιδωτή Στοά. 5. Νότια Είσοδος. 6. Νότιο Πρόπυλο. 7. Μεγάλη Σκάλα. 8. Διάδρομος των Αποθηκών. 9. Σκάλα. 10. Υπόστηλες Κρύπτες. 11. Αίθουσα του Θρόνου. 12. Τριμερές Ιερό. 13. Κεντρική Αυλή. 14. Διάδρομος Βόρειας Εισόδου. 15. «Τελωνείο». 16. «Θέατρο». 17. Μεγάλο Κλιμακοστάσιο. 18. Αίθουσα Διπλών Πελέκεων. 19. «Μέγαρο της Βασίλισσας». 20. Ιδιωτικά σπίτια. 21. Βόρεια Δεξαμενή Καθαρμών. 22. Θησαυροφυλάκια του Ιερού. 23. Ανατολικός Προμαχώνας. 24. Αποθήκες Γιγαντιαίων Πίθων. 25. Παλαιοανακτορικές αποθήκες.*

**The palace of Knossos. (plan C. Iliaki).**
*1. West Court. 2. West Porch. 3. Corridor of the Procession. 4. Stepped Portico. 5. South Entrance. 6. South Propylon. 7. Grand Staircase. 8. Long Corridor. 9. Stepped Porch. 10. Pillar Crypts. 11. Throne Room. 12. Tripartite Shrine. 13. Central Court. 14. North Entrance Passage. 15. «Customs House». 16. «Theatral Area». 17. Grand Staircase. 18. Hall of the Double Axes. 19. «Queen's Megaron». 20. Private houses. 21. North Lustral Basin. 22. Temple Repositories. 23. East Bastion. 24. Magazines of the Giant Pithoi. 25. Protopalatial magazines.*

**Le palais de Cnossos. (plan C. Iliaki).**
*1. Cour Occidentale. 2. Porche Ouest. 3. Corridor de la Procession. 4. Portique à degrés. 5. Entrée Sud. 6. Propylée Sud. 7. Grand Escalier. 8. Long Corridor. 9. Porche à degrés. 10. Cryptes hypostyles. 11. Salle du Trône. 12. Sanctuaire tripartite. 13. Cour Centrale. 14. Passage de l'entrée Nord. 15. «Douane». 16. «Théâtre». 17. Grand Escalier. 18. Hall des Doubles Haches. 19. «Mégaron de la Reine». 20. Maisons privées. 21. Bassin Nord de purification. 22. Trésor du Sanctuaire. 23. Bastion Est. 24. Magasins avec jarres géantes. 25. Magasins du Premier Palais.*

**Der Palast von Knossos. (Übersichtsskizze von K. Iliaki).**
*1. Westhof. 2. West-Propylon. 3. Prozessions - Korridor. 4. Stufenhalle. 5. Südeingang. 6. Süd-Propylon. 7. Große Treppe. 8. Korridor der Magazine. 9. Treppe. 10. Pfeiler-Krypten. 11. Thronsaal. 12. Dreiflügel-Heiligtum. 13. Mittelhof. 14. Korridor des N-Eingangs. 15. «Zollraum». 16. «Theater». 17. Großes Treppenhaus. 18. Halle der Doppeläxte. 19. «Mégaron der Königin». 20. Privathäuser. 21. N-Reinigungsbecken. 22. Schatzkammer des Heiligtums. 23. Ost-Bastion. 24. Magazine der Riesen-Pithoi. 25. Magazine der Altpalastzeit.*

**Il palazzo di Knossos. (dis C. Iliaki).**
*1. Cortile Ovest. 2. Propileo Ovest. 3. Corridoio della Processione. 4. Portico a gradinata. 5. Entrata Sud. 6. Propileo Sud. 7. Scala Grande. 8. Corridoio dei Magazzini. 9. Scala. 10. Cripte Ipóstile. 11. Stanza del Trono. 12. Santuario Tripartito. 13. Cortile Centrale. 14. Corridoio dell'Entrata Nord. 15. «Dogana». 16. «Teatro». 17. Grande Scala. 18. Sala delle Doppie Asce. 19. «Mégaron della Regina». 20. Case private. 21. Bacino Lustrale Nord. 22. Tesoro del Santuario. 23. Bastione Orientale. 24. Magazzini dei Pithoi giganti. 25. Magazzini dell'Antico Palazzo.*

8. Γενική άποψη του πρώτου ορόφου (Piano Nobile) της δυτικής πτέρυγας από τα βόρεια. Αριστερά, η Κεντρική Αυλή. Στο βάθος το βουνό Γιούκτας.

General view of the first floor (Piano Nobile) from the north. To the left the Central Court. In the background the Mount Juktas.

Vue générale du premier étage (Piano Nobile) du nord. A gauche la Cour Centrale. Au fond le Mont Jouktas.

Gesamtansicht des ersten Stockwerkes (Piano Nobile) des Westflügels. Links der Mittelhof. Im Hintergrund der Berg Jouctas.

Veduta generale, da nord, del Primo Piano ("Piano Nobile") dell'ala occidentale. A sinistra, il Cortile Centrale. In fondo, il Monte Juchtas.

9. Ο Διάδρομος της Πομπής που οδηγεί από τη Δυτική Είσοδο στο εσωτερικό του ανακτόρου. Στη μέση ένας «πομπικός δρόμος».

The Corridor of the Procession which leads from the West Porch to the inside of the palace. In the middle a "causeway".

Le Corridor de la Procession qui conduit du Porche Ouest à l'intérieur du palais. Au milieu une chaussée en relief.

Der Prozessionskorridor, der von dem Westeingang in das Innere des Palastes führt. In der Mitte ein Prozessionsweg.

Il Corridoio della Processione che dall'Entrata Ovest porta all'interno del Palazzo. Al centro, un passaggio rialzato detto "pompikòs dromos".

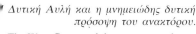

Δυτική Αυλή και η μνημειώδης δυτική πρόσοψη του ανακτόρου.

The West Court and the monumental west façade of the palace.

La Cour Occidentale et la façade Ouest monumentale du palais.

Der Westhof und die monumentale Westfassade des Palastes.

Il Cortile Ovest e la monumentale Facciata Occidentale del Palazzo.

11. Το Νότιο Πρόπυλο με αντίγραφα τμημάτων της Τοιχογραφίας της Πομπής.

The South Propylon with replicas of sections of the Procession Fresco.

Le Propylée Sud avec des reproductions des parties de la Fresque de la Procession.

Das Südpropylon mit Kopien von Teilen aus dem Prozessionsfresko.

Il Propileo Sud con una copia di alcune parti dell'Affresco della Processione.

12. Το μνημειώδες Νότιο Πρόπυλο και η Μεγάλη Σκάλα του πρώτου ορόφου.

The monumental South Propylon and the Grand Staircase of the upper storey.

Le Propylée Sud monumental et le Grand Escalier du premier étage.

Das monumentale Südpropylon und die Große Treppe des ersten Stockwerkes.

Il monumentale Propileo Sud e la Grande Scala del primo piano.

13. Ο «ρυτοφόρος»: μορφή
από την Τοιχογραφία της
Πομπής,
αντιπροσωπευτικός τύπος
Μινωίτη.
(Μουσείο Ηρακλείου).

"The Cup-Bearer": a
figure from the Procession
Fresco, a representative
type of a Minoan.
(Herakleion Museum).

"Le porteur de rhyton":
une figure de la Fresque de
la Procession, le type
représentatif du Minoen.
(Musée d'Hérakleion).

Der "Trichterträger": eine
Figur aus dem
Prozessionsfresko, einen
typischen Minoer
darstellend.
(Museum von Herakleion).

Il "Portatore del rhyton":
personaggio dell'Afresco
della Processione, tipica
figura di Minoico.
(Museo di Heraklion).

14. Η «Αίθουσα του Ιερού στόν πρώτο
όροφο (Piano Nobile) της δυτικής
πτέρυγας. Στο βάθος αναστηλωμένα
δωμάτια.

The "Sanctuary Hall" in the upper (Piano
Nobile) of the Wing. In the background
restored rooms.

Le "Hall-sanctuaire" au premier étage
(Piano Nobile) de l'aile Ouest. Au fond des
chambres restaurées.

Die "Halle des
Heiligtums" im
ersten Stock
(Piano Nobile)
des Westfügels.
Im Hintergrund
restaurierte
Räume.

La "Sala del
Santuario" al
primo piano
(Piano Nobile)
dell'ala
occidentale. In
fondo, alcune
stanze
restaurate.

15. *Τα μεγάλα ιερά κέρατα από πωρόλιθο κοντά στη Νότια Είσοδο.*

*The great limestone horns of consecration near the South Entrance.*

*Les doubles cornes en calcaire près de l'entrée Sud.*

*Die großen heiligen Konsekration - Hörner aus Porosstein in der Nähe des Südeingangs.*

*Le grandi corna Sacre in pietra porosa vicino all'Entrata Sud.*

16. Ο «Ιερεύς-Βασιλεύς» ή ο «πρίγκιπας με τα κρίνα». Ανάγλυφη τοιχογραφία. Το πρωτότυπο φυλάγεται στο Μουσείο Ηρακλείου.

"The Priest-King" or "The Prince of the Lilies". Relief fresco. The original is housed in the Herakleion Museum.

Le "Prêtre-roi" ou le "Prince aux fleurs de lys". Fresque en relief. L'original est au Musée d'Hérakleion.

Der "Priester-König" oder der "Lilienprinz". Relieffresko. Das Original befindet sich im Museum von Herakleion.

. Il "Re-Sacerdote" o il "Principe dei Gigli". Affresco a rilievo. L'originale è conservato nel Museo d'Heraklion.

18. Ο «Ναός - Τάφος».
(Αναπαράσταση Κ. Ηλιάκη).

The «Temple - Tomb».
(Reconstruction C. Iliacis).

La «Temple - tombeau».
(Reconstitution C. Iliacis).

Das «Tempelgrab».
(Rekonstruktion K. Iliakis).

La «Tomba - Santuario».
(Ricostruzione C. Iliacis).

19. Ο μεγάλος βασιλικός «Ναός - Τάφος» στη νότια άκρη της πόλης της Κνωσού.

The great royal "Temple - Tomb" at the south end of the town of Knossos.

Le grand "Temple - tombeau" royal à l'extremité Sud de la ville de Cnosos.

Das große königliche "Tempelgrab" am Südende der Stadt von Knossos.

La grande e regale "Tomba - Santuario", all'estremità sud della Città di Cnosso.

αναπαράσταση
ς Βαθμιδωτής
οάς.
ναπαράστα-
Κ. Ηλιάκη).

construction
the Stepped
rtico.
econstruction
Iliaci).

constitution
a façade
est de la
ur Centrale.
constitution
Iliaci).

konstruktion
Gestuften
a.
kostruktion
Iliaki).

ostruzione
Portico a
dinata.
ostruzione
liaci).

*Αναπαράσταση του Καραβανσεράι (κατά τον Έβανς).*
*Reconstitution of the Caravanserai. (After Evans).*
*Reconstitution du Caravansérail. (D'après Evans).*
*Wiederherstellung der Karawanserei. (Nach Evans).*
*Disegno ricostruttivo del "Caravanserraglio". (Secondo Evans).*

22. *Αναπαράσταση της δυτικής πλευράς της Κεντρικής Αυλής.*
*(Αναπαράσταση Κ. Ηλιάκη)*

*Reconstruction of the west side of the Central Court.*
*(Reconstruction C. Iliacis).*

*Reconstitution de la côté Ouest de la Cour Centrale.*
*(Reconstitution C. Iliacis).*

*Rekonstruktion der Westseite des Mittelhofes.*
*(Rekonstruktion K. Iliakis).*

*Disegno ricostruzione del lato occidentale del Cortile centrale.*
*(Ricostruzione C. Iliacis).*

*Η τοιχογραφία με τις πέρδικες από το «Καραβανσεράι». Τα στρογγυλά αντικείμενα παριστάνουν φλεβωτές πέτρες. Το μεγαλύτερο τμήμα της τοιχογραφίας είναι συμπληρωμένο. (Μουσείο Ηρακλείου).*

*The Partridge Fresco from the "Caravanserai". The round objects represent veined pebbles. The largest part of the fresco is restored. (Herakleion Museum).*

*La fresque aux perdrix du "Caravansérail". Les objets ronds représentent des cailloux veinés. La plus grande partie de la fresque est restaurée. (Musée d'Hérakleion).*

*Das Fresko mit den Rebhühnern aus der Karawanserei. Die runden Gegenstände stellen geäderte Steine dar. Der grösste Teil des Freskos ist ergänzt. (Museum von Herakleion).*

*L'Affresco con le Pernici proveniente dal "Caravanserraglio". Gli oggetti rotondi raffigurano pietre variegate. La maggior parte dell'Affresco è restaurata. (Museo di Heraklion).*

▶

23. *Η Αίθουσα του Θρόνου με την Τοιχογραφία των Γρυπών.*

*The Throne Room with the Griffin Fresco.*

*La Salle du Trône avec la fresque des griffons.*

*Der Thronsaal mit dem Greifenfresko.*

*La Stanza del Trono con l'Affresco dei Grifoni.*

*Ο προθάλαμος της Αίθουσας του Θρόνου με μια λεκάνη από πορφυρίτη, ίσως για αγιασμό.*

The antechamber of the Throne Room with a porphyry basin, perhaps for holy water.

*L'antichambre de la Salle du Trône avec un bassin de porphyre, peut-être pour être rempli d'eau bénite.*

*Der Vorraum des Thronsaales mit einem Porphyrbecken, vielleicht für Weihwasser.*

*L'Anticamera della Stanza del Torno con un bacile di pietra di porfido, usato forse per aspersioni sacre.*

26. *Υπόστυλες κρύπτες της δυτικής πτέρυγας.*

Pillar Crypts of the west wing.

*Les cryptes hypostyles le l'aile Ouest.*

Pfeilerkrypten des Westflügels.

*Cripte ipóstile dell'ala occidentale.*

*Αναστηλωμένος φωταγωγός του πρώτου ορόφου της δυτικής πτέρυγας με αναπαραστάσεις τοιχογραφιών.*

Restored ligh-well of the upper storey of the West Wing with replicas of frescoes.

*Puits de lumière restauré du premier étage de l'aile Ouest avec des reproductions des fresques.*

Restaurierter Lichthof des ersten Stockwerkes des Westflügels mit wiederhergestellten Fresken.

*Lucernario restaurato al primo piano dell'ala occidentale, con copie di affreschi.*

27. Η «Αποθήκη του Ψηλού Πίθου» στη δυτική πτέρυγα του ανακτόρου. Ο τεράστιος αυτός πίθος έχει διακόσμηση ιδιαίτερα πλούσια.

*The "Room of the Tall Pithos" in the West Wing of the palace. This huge jar has a very rich decoration.*

*La "Chambre du haut pithos" à l'aile Ouest du palais. Cette jarre énorme a un décor très riche.*

*Das "Magazin des Hohen Pithos" im Westflügel des Palastes. Dieser gewaltige Pithos hat eine besonders reiche Verzierung.*

*Il "Magazzino dell'alto Pithos" nell'ala occidentale del Palazzo. Questo enorme vaso ha una decorazione particolarmente ricca.*

28. «Το Γαλάζ[ Πουλί». Τοιχογραφ[ από το «Σπίτι τ[ Τοιχογραφιών[ (Μουσείο Ηρακλείο[

*Blue Bird Fresco fro[ the "House of t[ Frescoe[ (Herakleion Museum[*

*La fresque à l'oise[ bleu de la "Maison d[ Fresque[ (Musée d'Héraklei[*

*"Der blaue Voge[ Fresko aus dem "Ha[ der Fresker[ (Museum v[ Heraklei[*

*L'"Uccello azzurr[ Affresco provenier[ dalla "Casa de[ Affresch[ (Museo di Heraklio[*

29. Αποθήκη[ δυτικής πτέρυγας[ πίθους και κασέλες [ πάτω[

*Magazine of the W[ Wing, with pithoi [ sunken cists in the fl[*

*Magasin de l'aile Ou[ avec des pithoi et [ cistes enfoncées au [*

*Magazin des Westflü[ mit Pithoi [ Einlassungen im Bo[*

*Magazzino dell[ occidentale con pith[ "casselle" [ pavime[*

30. Μεγάλο Κλιμακοστάσιο της ανατολικής πτέρυγας. Η «Βεράντα της Βασιλικής Φρουράς». Στο βάθος αντίγραφο τοιχογραφίας με οκτώσχημες ασπίδες.

*Grand Staircase of the East Wing: The "Veranda of the Royal Guard". In the background a replica of the fresco with figure-of-eight shields.*

*Le Grand Escalier de l'aile Ouest: La "véranda de la garde royale". Au fond une copie de la fresque de boucliers en forme d'huit.*

*Großes Treppenhaus des Ostflügels: Die "Veranda der Königswache". Im Hintergrund Kopien des Freskos mit den achtförmigen Schilden.*

*La Grande Scala dell'ala orientale: la "Veranda della guardia Reale". Sul fondo copia dell'affresco raffigurante scudi a forma di otto.*

31. Μεγάλο Κλιμακοστάσιο της ανατολικής πτέρυγας: Η Αίθουσα των Κιονοστοιχιών.

Grand Staircase of the East Wing: The Hall of the Colonnades.

Grand Escalier de l'aile Est: Le Hall des Colonnades.

Großes Treppenhaus des Ostflügels: Die Säulenhalle.

La Grande Scala dell'ala orientale: la Sala del Peristilio.

32. Το «Μέγαρο της Βασίλισσας». Η τοιχογραφία των Δελφινιών.
   The "Queen's Megaron". The Dolphin Fresco.
   Le "Mégaron de la Reine". La Fresque aux Daulphins.
   Das "Megaron der Königin". Das Delphinefresko.
   Il "Mégaron della Regina". L'Affresco dei Delfini.

33. Η Τοιχογραφία των Δελφινιών από το «Μέγαρο της Βασίλισσας». Η εικόνα αυτή εκφράζει την αγάπη των Μινωιτών για τη θάλασσα. (Μουσείο Ηρακλείου).

The Dolphin Fresco from the "Queen's Megaron". This picture expresses the love of the Minoans for the sea. (Herakleion Museum).

La fresque aux dauphins du "Mégaron de la Reine". Cette image exprime l'amour des Minoens pour la mer. (Musée d'Hérakleion).

Das Delphinenfresko aus dem "Megaron der Königin". Dieses Gemälde zeigt die Liebe der Minoer für das Meer. (Museum von Herakleion).

L'Affresco dei Delfini proveniente dal "Mégaron della Regina". Questa pittura manifesta l'amore dei Minoici per il mare. (Museo di Heraklion).

Η Τοιχογραφία της Χορεύτριας
ό το «Μέγαρο της Βασίλισσας».
(Μουσείο Ηρακλείου).

Girl Dancer Fresco from the
"Queen's Megaron".
(Herakleion Museum).

La fresque de la Danseuse du
"Mégaron de la Reine".
(Musée d'Hérakleion).

Das Fresko der Tänzerin aus dem
"Megaron der Königin".
(Museum von Herakleion).

resco della Ballerina proveniente
dal "Mégaron della Regina".
(Museo di Heraklion).

35. Το «Μέγαρο της Βασίλισσας» και ο φωταγωγός του.
The "Queen's Megaron" and its light-well.
Le "Mégaron de la Reine" et son puits de lumière.
Das "Megaron der Königin" und sein Lichthof.
Il "Mégaron della Regina" con il suo lucernario.

36 Το λουτρό του
«Μεγάρου της
Βασίλισσας»
(κατά τον Έβανς).

The bathroom of the
"Queen's Megaron".
(After Evans).

Le salle de bain du
"Megaron de la Reine".
(D'après Evans).

Das Bad des «Megaron
der Königin».
(Nach Evans).

"Mégaron della Regina":
la camera da bagno.
(Secondo Evans).

37. Το «Μέγαρο της
Βασίλισσας».
(Κατά τον Έβανς).

"Quenn's Megaron".
(After Evans).

Le "Megaron de la
Reine".
(D'après Evans).

Das «Megaron der
Königin».
(Nach Evans).

Il "Mégaron della
Regina".
(Secondo Evans).

38. Ιερό των Διπλών
Πελέκεων.
(Αναπαράσταση
Κ. Ηλιάκη).

Sanctuary of the Double
Axes. (Reconstruction
C. Iliacis).

Le Santcuaire des Doubles
Haches.
(Reconstitution C. Iliacis).

Heiligtum der Doppeläxte.
(Rekonstruktion
K. Iliakis).

Planimetria del Santuario
delle doppie asce.
(Ricostruzione C. Iliacis).

39. Αίθουσα των Διπλών
Πελέκεων.
(Κατά τον Έβανς).

Hall of the Double Axes.
(After Evans).

Le Hall des Doubles
Haches.
(D'après Evans).

Halle der Doppeläxte.
(Nach Evans).

Sala delle doppie asce.
(Secondo Evans).

41. Η μερικά αναστηλωμένη δυτική στοά του Διαδρόμου της Βόρειας Εισόδου με την Τοιχογραφία του Ταύρου.

The partly restored west portico of the North Entrance Passage with the relief fresco of the charging bull.

Le portique Ouest, en partie restauré, du Passage de l'entrée Nord, avec la fresque en relief du taureau chargeant.

Die zum Teil wiederhergestellte Weststoa des Korridors des Nordeingangs mit dem Stuckrelief des Stieres.

Il Portico Ovest del Corridoio dell'Entrata Nord, parzialmente restaurato, con l'Affresco del Toro.

Ο Διάδρομος της Βόρειας Εισόδου. (Κατά τον Έβανς).

North Entrance Passage. (After Evans).

Le Passage de l'Entrée Nord. (D'après Evans).

Korridor des Nordeinganges. (Nach Evans).

Il Corridoio dell'Entrata Nord. (Secondo Evans).

42. Το «Τελωνείο» και η Βόρεια Είσοδος με την ανάγλυφη
Τοιχογραφία του Ταύρου.

*"Customs' House" and the North Entrance with the relief
fresco of the charging bull.*

*La "Douane" et l'entrée Nord avec la fresque en
relief du taureau chargeant.*

*Die "Zollstelle" und der Nordeingang mit dem Stuckrelief
des Stieres.*

*La "Dogana" ed Entrata Nord con l'Affresco a
rilievo del Toro.*

43. Γενική άποψη του «Θεάτρου» του ανακτόρου. Διακρίνονται δύο «πομπικοί δρόμοι».
General view of the "Theatral Area" of the palace, with two "causeways".
Vue générale de l'"Aire théâtrale", avec deux chaussées en relief.
Gesamtansicht des "Theaters" des Palastes, auf der zwei Prozessionswege erkennbar sind.
Veduta generale del "Teatro" del Palazzo. Si distinguono due passaggi rialzati.

44. Ο Διάδρομος της Βόρειας Εισόδου και στο βάθος η Βόρεια Δεξαμενή Καθαρμών.

North Entrance Passage and North Lustral Area in the background.

Le Passage de l'entrée Nord et au fond le Bassin Nord de purification.

Der Weg des Nordeingangs im Hintergrund mit dem nördlichen Kultbassin.

Corridoio dell' Entrata Nord e, sul fondo, il Bacino Lustrale Nord.

45. Η «Βασιλική Οδός» που συνδέει το «θέατρο» με το Μικρό Ανάκτορο.

The "Royal Road" connecting the "Theatral Area" with the Little Palace.

La "Route Royale" qui relie l'"Aire théâtrale" avec le Petit Palais.

Die "Königstraße", die das "Theater" mit dem Kleinen Palast verbindet.

La "Via Reale" che unisce il "Teatro" al Piccolo Palazzo.

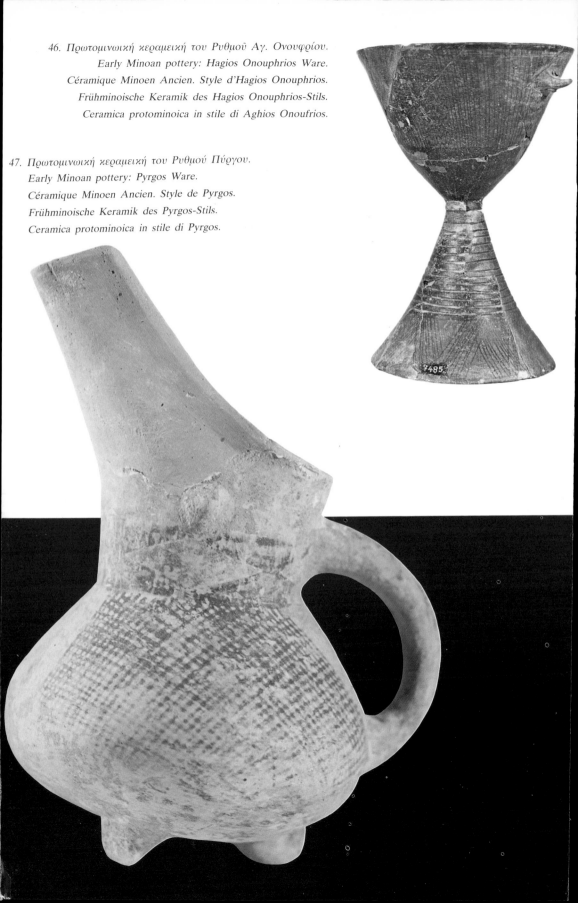

46. Πρωτομινωική κεραμεική του Ρυθμού Αγ. Ονουφρίου.
   Early Minoan pottery: Hagios Onouphrios Ware.
   Céramique Minoen Ancien. Style d'Hagios Onouphrios.
   Frühminoische Keramik des Hagios Onouphrios-Stils.
   Ceramica protominoica in stile di Aghios Onoufrios.

47. Πρωτομινωική κεραμεική του Ρυθμού Πύργου.
   Early Minoan pottery: Pyrgos Ware.
   Céramique Minoen Ancien. Style de Pyrgos.
   Frühminoische Keramik des Pyrgos-Stils.
   Ceramica protominoica in stile di Pyrgos.

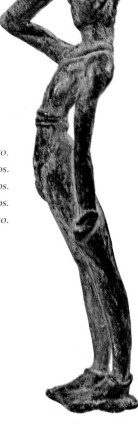

8. Χρυσό δαχτυλίδι με θρησκευτική
σκηνή από τα Ισόπατα.

*Gold signet ring with a religious
scene from Isopata.*

*Bague en or portant une
représentation religieuse. Isopata.*

*Goldring mit einer religiösen
Szene aus Isopata.*

*Anello d'oro con una scena religiosa
proveniente da Isopata.*

49. Χάλκινος λάτρης από την Τύλισο.

*Bronze worshipper from Tylissos.*

*Adorant de bronze. Tylissos.*

*Adorant aus Bronze aus Tylissos.*

*Adorante in rame di Tilisso.*

Χρυσοί διπλοί πελέκεις από το ιερό σπήλαιο στο Αρκαλοχώρι.
*Gold double axes from the sacred cave of Arkalochori.*
*Doubles haches en or. Grotte sacrée d'Arkalochori.*
*Goldene Doppeläxte aus der Kultgrotte von Arkalochori.*
*Duplici accette d'oro dalla sacra grotta di Arcalochori.*

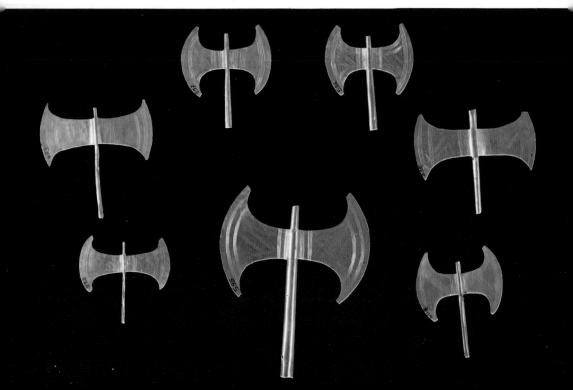

51. *Λίθινη πυξίδα από τη Μαρωνιά κοντά στη Σητεία. Προανακτορική εποχή.*

*Stone pyxis from Maronia, near Siteia. Pre-palatial period.*

*Coffret en pierre de Maronia près de Sitia. Époque prépalatiale.*

*Steinerne Pyxis (Dose) aus Maronias in der Nähe von Seteia (Sitia). Vorpalastzeit.*

*Pyxis di pietra proveniente da Maronià vicino a Sitia. Epoca prepalaziale.*

52. *Πρωτομινωικά χρυσά κοσμήματα από το νεκροταφείο του Μόχλου.*

*Early Minoan gold jewellery from the cemetery of Mochlos.*

*Bijoux en or Minoen Ancien du cimetière de Mochlos.*

*Frühminoischer Goldschmuck aus der Nekropole von Mochlos.*

*Gioielli d'oro protominoici provenienti dal cimitero di Mochlos.*

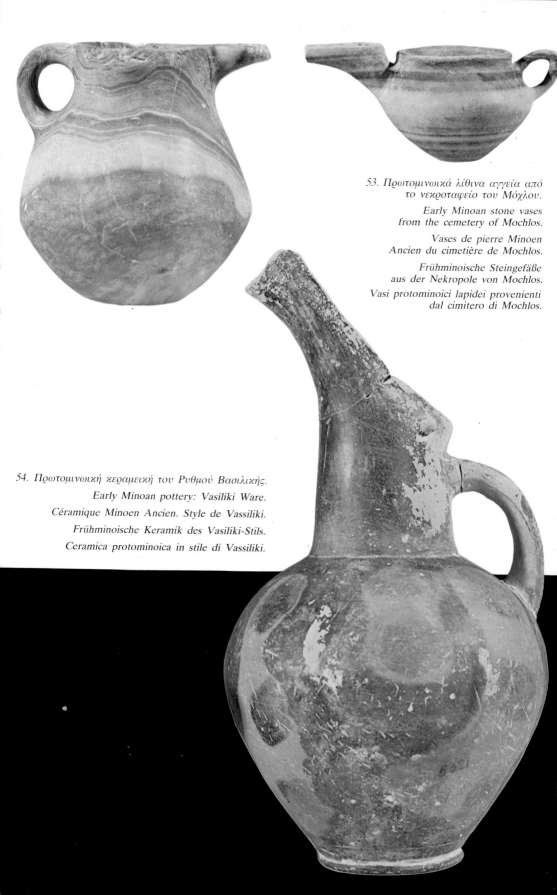

53. Πρωτομινωικά λίθινα αγγεία από
το νεκροταφείο του Μόχλου.

Early Minoan stone vases
from the cemetery of Mochlos.

Vases de pierre Minoen
Ancien du cimetière de Mochlos.

Frühminoische Steingefäße
aus der Nekropole von Mochlos.

Vasi protominoici lapidei provenienti
dal cimitero di Mochlos.

54. Πρωτομινωική κεραμεική του Ρυθμού Βασιλικής.

Early Minoan pottery: Vasiliki Ware.

Céramique Minoen Ancien. Style de Vassiliki.

Frühminoische Keramik des Vasiliki-Stils.

Ceramica protominoica in stile di Vassiliki.

55. Καταστόλιστη οπω-
ροδόχη Καμαραϊκού
Ρυθμού από τη Φαιστό.

All-over painted
fruitstand of the
Kamares Style from
Phaistos.

Fruitier du Style de
Kamarès. Phaistos.

Reich verzierte
Obstschale des
Kamares-Stils aus
Phaistos.

Fruttiera completamente
decorata in stile di
Kamares proveniente
da Festò.

56. Κρατηρόσχημο αγγείο
Καμαραϊκού Ρυθμού
από τη Φαιστό.

Krater of the Kamares
Style from Phaistos.

Cratère du Style de
Kamarès. Phaistos.

Kraterartiges Gefäß des
Kamares-Stils aus Phaist

Vaso a forma di cratere
stile di Kamares proven
da Festò.

57. Πρόχους
του
Καμαραϊκού
Ρυθμού από
τη Φαιστό.

Jug of the
Kamares Style
from Phaistos.

Cruche du Style
de Kamarès.
Phaistos.

Kanne des
Kamares-Stils
aus Phaistos.

Prochous (stile
di Kamares)
proveniente
da Festò.

58. Ο Δίσκος
της Φαιστού.

The Phaistos
Disk.

Le Disque
de Phaistos.

Der Diskos
von Phaistos.

Il Disco
di Festò.

59. Πλακίδιο από φαγεντιανή με αγελάδα που θηλάζει το μοσχάρι της. Από την Κνωσό.
Faience plaque with a cow suckling her calf From Knossos.
Plaque en faience représentant une vache allaitant son petit. Knossos.
Fayencetäfelchen mit einer Kuh und ihrem säugenden Kalb. Aus Knossos.
Tavolette di ceramica con una mucca allattante il suo vitello; provenienti da Cnosso.

σό εξάρτημα μελισσών
από τα Μάλια.

*Gold bee pendant
from Malia.*

*Pendentif aux abeilles,
en or. Malia.*

*ldener Bienenanhänger
aus Malia.*

*Pendente d'oro con api
proveniente da Malia.*

61. Λίθινος πέλεκυς σε σχήμα πάνθηρα. Από τα Μάλια.

*Axe in the form of a panther. From Malia.*

*Hache en forme de panthère. Provenance: Malia.*

*Axt in Pantherform. Aus Malia.*

*Accetta reale che termina in una pantera proveniente da Malia.*

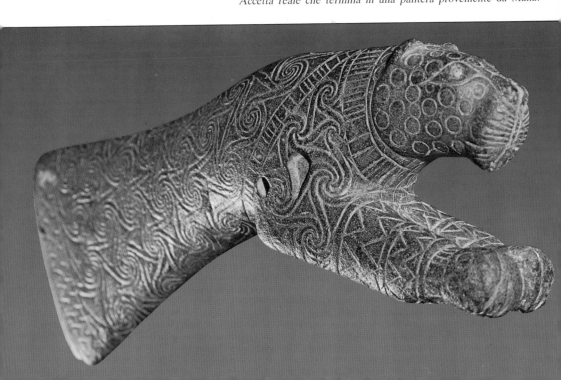

62. Οι θεές των όφεων από φαγεντιανή. Από την Κνωσό.

*Faience Snake Goddesses. From Knossos.*

*Déesses aux serpents, en faïence. Cnossos.*

*Die Schlangengöttinnen. Fayence. Aus Knossos.*

*Le Dee dei Serpenti in maiolica Tesoriere dei Santuario. Di Cnosso.*

64. Φτερωτοί ιεροί γρύπες. Ανάγλυφη τοιχογραφία από τον πρώ
όροφο της ανατολικής πτέρυγα
Ανάκτορο Κνωσό

*Winged sacral griffins. Relief fresco from the first floor of the Ea*
*Wing. Palace of Knoss*

*Griffons sacrés ailés. Fresque en relief du premier étage de l'aile E*
*Palais de Cnosso*

*Geflügelte heilige Greifen. Relieffresko aus dem ersten Stock d*
*Ostflügels. Palast von Knoss*

*Sacri Grifoni Alati. Affresco a rilievo proveniente dal primo pia*
*dell'ala orientale. Palazzo di Cnoss*

Η αιώρησῃ: πήλινο ομοίωμα.
από την Αγία Τριάδα.

The Swinging Woman:
clay model from Hagia Triada.

Le balancement: maquette
en terre cuite d'Hagia Triada.

Schaukel: Nachbildung
aus Ton aus Hagia Triada.

Il dondolamento: simulacro
fittile di Aghia Triada.

66. Ρυτό από λευκό ασβεστόλιθο σε σχήμα κεφαλιού λέαινας. Ανάκτορο Κνωσσού.

*Rhyton of white limestone in form of a lioness' head. Palace of Knossos.*

*Rhyton en calcaire blanc en forme de tête de lionne. Palais de Cnossos.*

*Rhyton aus weißem Kalkstein im Form des Kopfes einer Löwin. Palast von Knossos.*

*Rhyton di pietra calcarea bianca a testa di leonessa. Palazzo di Cnosso.*

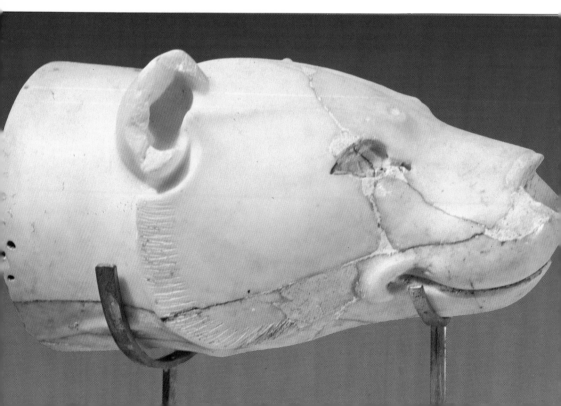

Πινακίδες της Γραμμικής γραφής Β από την Κνωσό.
Tablets with Linear B script from Knossos.
Tablettes en Linéaire B. Knossos.
Tafeln mit der Linearschrift B aus Knossos.
Tavole con scrittura Lineare B da Cnosso.

67. Ιερός κόμβος από ελεφαντόδοντο.
Ανάκτορο της Κνωσού.
Ivory sacral knot. Palace of Knossos.
Noeud sacré en ivoire. Palais de Cnossos.
Sakraler Knoten aus Elfenbein. Palast von Knossos.
Sacro nodo di avorio. Palazzo di Cnosso.

Ακροβάτης από ελεφαντόδοντο, από σκηνή ταυρομαχίας. Από την Κνωσό.
Ivory acrobat, from a bull-game scene. From Knossos.
Acrobate en ivoire provenant d'une scène de tauromachie. Cnossos.
Akrobat aus Elfenbein von einer Stierspielszene. Aus Knossos.
Acrobata in avorio da una scena di tauromachia. Di Cnosso.

69. Πήλινος κάλαθος με διπλούς πελέκεις από την Ψείρα.

Clay basketvase with double axes from Pseira.

Kalathos de terre cuite portant une représentation de doubles haches. Pseira.

Korbgefäß aus Ton mit Doppeläxten von Pseira.

Cestino fittile con duplici accette di Pseira.

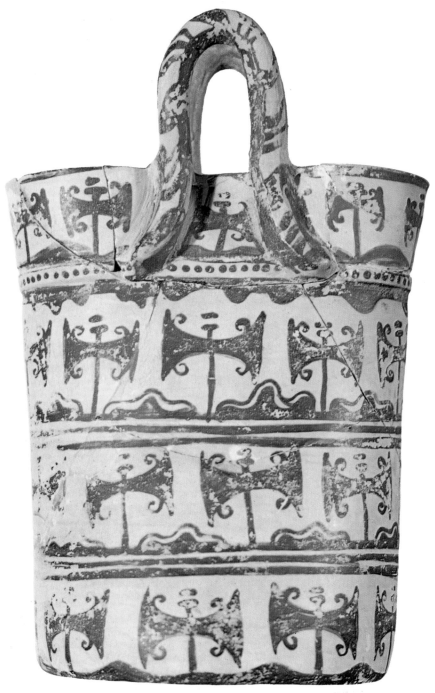

70. Κράνος από
χαυλιόδοντες
κάπρου, μερικά
συμπληρωμένο.
Από Ζαφέρ
Παπούρα,
Κνωσός.

r's-tusk helmet,
partly restored.
From Zapher
roura, Knossos.

Casque en dents
de sanglier,
lement restauré.
venance: Zapher
Papoura,
Cnossos.

Eberzahnhelm,
um Teil ergäntz.
Aus Zapher
poura, Knossos.

Elmo fatto di
nne di cinghiale
parzialmente
restaurato.

Μετανακτορική
ινη σαρκοφάγος
από τα Βασιλικά
Ανώγεια.

Postpalatial clay
coffin from
Vasilika Anogeia.

cophage en terre
cuite Postpalatial.
Vasilika Anogeia.

Tonsarkophag der
Nachpalastzeit aus
Vasilika Anogeia.

Sacrofago fittile
postpalaziale di
Vassilikà Anoghia.

72. Η «πρόχους» των «καλαμοειδών» από τη Φαιστό. Φυτικός Ρυθμός.

The "Jug of the Reeds" from Phaistos. Floral style.

La "cruche aux roseaux" Phaistos. Style Floral.

Schnabelkanne mit Schilfdekor aus Phaistos im Florastil.

La "prochous delle canne" di Festò. Stile vegetale.

73. Λέαινα κατασπαράζει ταύρο. Σφραγίδα από την Κνωσό με το εκμαγείο της.

Lioness devouring a bull. Seal from Knossos with its cast.

Lionne dévorant un taureau. Sceau de Cnossos avec son empreinte.

Löwin einen Stier zerreißend. Siegel aus Knossos mit seinem Abdruck.

Una leonessa sbrana un toro. Sigillo di Cnosso con il suo calco.

74. Θεά πλαισιωμένη από γρύπες. Σφραγίδα από την Κνωσό με το εκμαγείο της.

Goddess flanked by griffins. Seal from Knossos with its cast.

Déesse flanquée de griffons. Sceau de Cnossos avec son empreinte.

Göttin umgeben von Greifen. Siegel aus Knossos mit seinem Abdruck.

Dea tra grifoni. Sigillo di Cnoso con il suo calco.

76. *Φλασκί του Θαλάσσιου Ρυθμού από το Παλαίκαστρο.*
   *Marine Style flask from Palaikastro.*
   *Flacon du Style marin. Palaikastro.*
   *"Pilgerflasche" im Meeresstil aus Palaikastro.*
   *Fiasca in stile marino di Palaicastro.*

77. Ελεφάντινο πλακίδιο με φανταστικό πουλί.
Από το Παλαίκαστρο.

Ivory plaque with an imaginary bird.
From Palaikastro.

Plaquette en ivoire avec un oiseau fantastique.
Palaikastro.

Elfenbeintäfelchen mit Plantasievogel.
Aus Palaikastro.

Tavoletta di avorio con un uccello fantastico
di Palaicastro.

78. Πήλινα ειδώλια λυράρη και χορευτριών.
Από το Παλαίκαστρο.

Clay idols of a lyreplayer and dancing women.
From Palaikastro.

Figurines en terre cuite. Joueur de lyre et femmes dancantes.
Provenance: Palaikastro.

Idole aus Ton. Lyraspieler und tanzende Frauen.
Aus Palaikastro.

Gruppo di danzatori in argilla proveniente
di Palaicastro.

79. Το κύπελλο της Αναφοράς ή του Αρχηγού
   από την Αγία Τριάδα.

The Chieftain Cup, from Hagia Triada.

Le Gobelet du Chef. Hagia Triada.

"Paradebecher" bezw. "Prinzenbecher"
aus Hagia Triada.

La coppa del Memoriale o del Capo
proveniente da Aghia Triada.

80. Το αγγείο των Θεριστών,
   από την Αγία Τριάδα.
The Harvester Vase, from Hagia Triada.
e Vase des Moissonneurs. Hagia Triada.
Schnittervase aus Hagia Triada.
Il vaso dei Falciatori di Aghia Triada.

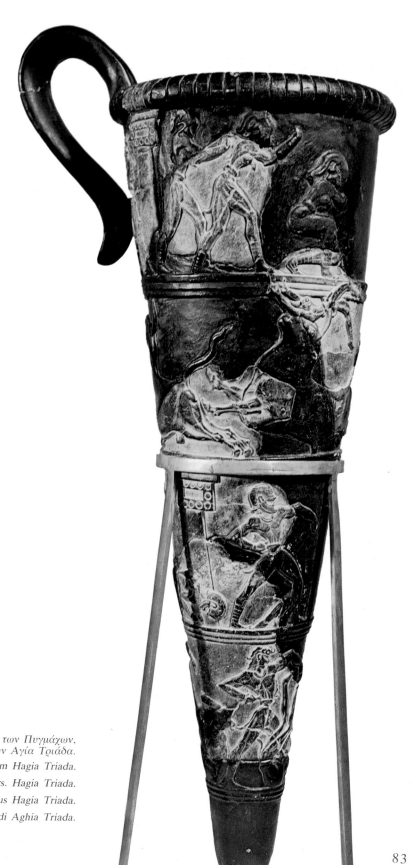

81. Το Ρυτό των Πυγμάχων,
   από την Αγία Τριάδα.
The Boxer Vase, from Hagia Triada.
Le Rhyton des Boxeurs. Hagia Triada.
Faustkämpfer-Rhyton aus Hagia Triada.
Il rhyton dei Pugilatori di Aghia Triada.

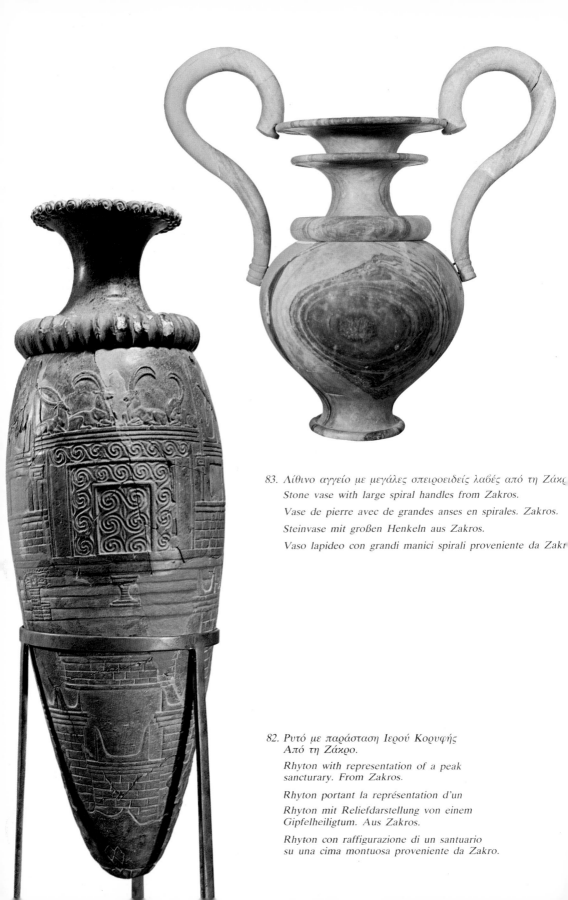

83. Λίθινο αγγείο με μεγάλες σπειροειδείς λαβές από τη Ζάκρο
    Stone vase with large spiral handles from Zakros.
    Vase de pierre avec de grandes anses en spirales. Zakros.
    Steinvase mit großen Henkeln aus Zakros.
    Vaso lapideo con grandi manici spirali proveniente da Zakro

82. Ρυτό με παράσταση Ιερού Κορυφής
    Από τη Ζάκρο.
    Rhyton with representation of a peak
    sancturary. From Zakros.
    Rhyton portant la représentation d'un
    Rhyton mit Reliefdarstellung von einem
    Gipfelheiligtum. Aus Zakros.
    Rhyton con raffigurazione di un santuario
    su una cima montuosa proveniente da Zakro.

84. Δισκοπότηρο της αγίας κοινωνίας από στιγμωτό οψιανό. Από τη Ζάκρο.

Chalice of spotted obsidian for the sacred communion. From Zakros.

Calice en obsidienne mouchetée destiné à la communion. Zakros.

Kultkelch aus geflecktem Obsidian aus Zakros.

Calice sacro di Santa Comunione in ossidiana macchiata proveniente da Zakro.

85. Μεσομινωικά ειδώλια λάτρεων από το Ιερό Κορυφής του Πετσοφά.

Middle Minoan cult figurines from the Peak Sanctuary of Petsophas.

Figurines d'adorants provenant du Sanctuaire de Sommet de Petsopha. Minoen Moyen.

Mittelminoische Idole von Adoranten aus dem Gipfelheiligtum von Petsophas.

Statuette mediominoiche di adoratori del Santuario Santuario di Korifi a Petsofà.

86. Πίθος Ανακτορικού Ρυθμού με διπλούς πελέκεις, από την Κνωσό.

Palace Style pithos with double axes from Knossos.

Pithos avec doubles haches. Style du Palais. Cnossos.

Pithos des Palast-Stils mit Doppeläxten aus Knossos.

Giara di stile palaziale con duplici accette. Cnosso.

87. Το
ταυροκέφαλο
ρυτό. Από το
Μικρό
Ανάκτορο
της Κνωσού.

Bull's head
rhyton. From
the Little
Palace
of Knossos.

Rhyton en
forme de tête
de taureau.
Cnossos, Petit
Palais.

Stierkopf-
Rhyton aus
dem Kleinen
Palast
von Knossos.

Il rhyton a testa
di toro. Piccolo
Palazzo
di Cnosso.

88. *Κομψή σπονδική*
*πρόχους. Από ένα*
*τάφο στον*
*Κατσαμπά.*

*Elegant libation jug.*
*From a tomb at*
*Katsambas.*

*Cruche à libations.*
*Tombe de*
*Katsamba.*

*Zierliche*
*Opferkanne aus*
*einem Grab in*
*Katsambas.*

*Delicata prochous*
*libatoria*
*proveniente da una*
*tomba di Katsambà.*

89. Η Θεά με τις Παπαρούνες από το Γάζι. 13ος π.Χ. αι.

The Goddess with the Poppies from Gazi. 13th c. B.C.

La Déesse aux pavots. Gazi. XIIIe s. av. J.-C.

Die Mogngöttin aus Gazi. 13. Jhdt. v. Chr.

La Dea con i Papaveri. Sec. XIII a. C.

*Σαρκοφάγος Αγίας Τριάδας: σπονδή και προσφορές στο νεκρό.*

Sarcophagus from Hagia Triada: libation and offerings to the dead man.

Sarcophage d'Hagia Triada: libations et offrandes au défunt.

Sarkophag aus Hagia Triada: Spenden und Opfergaben an den Toten.

Sacrofago di Aghia Triada: libazione e offerte al morto.

92. *Σαρκοφάγος Αγίας Τριάδας: μυθικό άρμα με θεές.*

Sarcophagus from Hagia Triada: mythical chariot with goddesses.

Sarcophage d'Hagia Triada: char mythique avec des déesses.

Sarkophag aus Hagia Triada: mythisches Gespann mit Göttinnen.

Sacrofago di Aghia Triada: carro mitico con dee.

*. Σαρκοφάγος Αγίας Τριάδας: θυσία ταύρου.*

Sarcophagus from Hagia Triada: bull sacrifice.

Sarcophage d'Hagia Triada: sacrifice du taureau.

Sarkophag aus Hagia Triada: Stieropfer.

Sacrofago di Aghia Triada: il sacrificio di un toro.

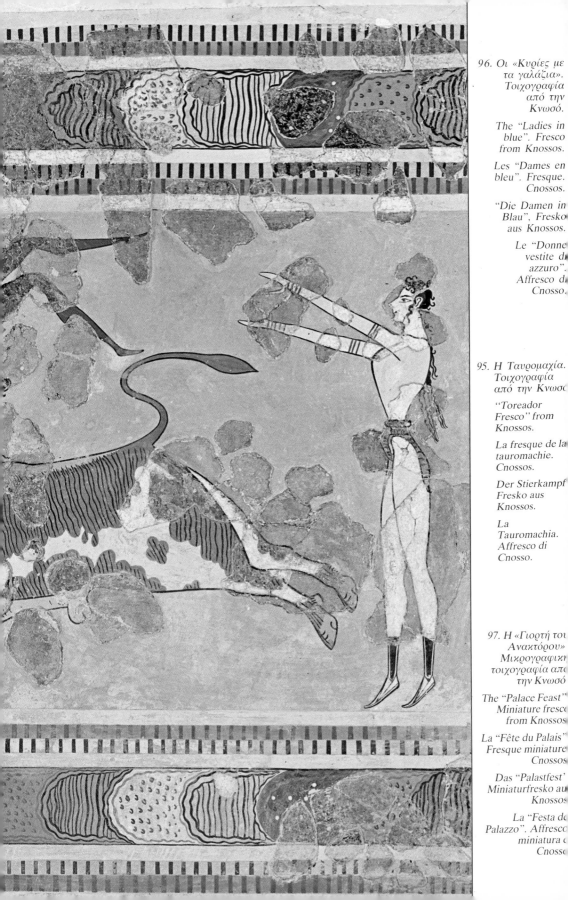